श्रीमद्भगवद्गीता

पञ्चदशोऽध्यायः - पुरुषोत्तमयोगः

śrīmadbhagavadgītā

pañcadaśo'dhyāyaḥ - puruṣottamayogaḥ

Bhagavad-Gītā Chapter Fifteen

Sanskrit Text with Transliteration, Translation & Brief Commentary

गीता मूलं १५

Gītā Mūlaṁ 15

गीता या मधुसूदनप्रभविणी युक्ता परं ब्रह्मणि
gītā yā madhusūdana-prabhaviṇī yuktā paraṁ brahmaṇi
या कृष्णेन कृताऽखिलं नयनवद् वक्षोऽतिगूढार्थिनी ।
yā kṛṣṇena kṛtā-'khilaṃ nayanavad vakṣo-'tigūḍhārthinī ,
या लोकत्रयस्य मार्गविधिनी धर्मस्य साक्षात्पथा
yā lokatrayasya marga-vidhinī dharmasya sākṣāt-pathā ,
सा श्रीकृष्णमुखारविन्दजनिता तस्याः मूलं प्रयच्छामि ॥
sā śrī-kṛṣṇa-mukhāravinda-janitā tasyāḥ mūlaṁ prayacchāmi .

That Gītā—which's born from Madhusūdana -- who exists in Oneness with Braham;
that Gītā—which's uttered by Krishna -- of profound visions of deep mysteries concealed within;
that Gītā—which lights the Dharma-path across the threefold world;
that Gītā—that sprung from Shri Krishna's lotus-lips
—to Her sacred roots I proceed and take refuge.

Belongs to ______________________

॥ यतो धर्मस्ततो जयः - एकं-सनातन-धर्म विजयः ॥
- yato dharmastato jayaḥ -- ekaṁ sanātana-dharma vijayaḥ -
- Where Dharma abides Victory abides -- Victory unto Ekam-Sanātana-Dharma -

Published by: only **RAMA** only
(an Imprint of Vijay Saxena)

Title: **Gita Mūlaṁ 15 – Bhagavad Gita Chapter Fifteen**
Sub-Title: **Sanskrit Text with Transliteration, Translation & Brief Commentary**
A No-Opinions Commentary. Only Facts. Bhagavad-Gitā As It Truly Is.
An Excellent Resource for Sectless Gitā-Study (With Wide Margin for Taking Notes)

गीता मूलं १५
gītā mūlaṁ 15
श्रीमद्भगवद्गीता पञ्चदशोऽध्यायः - पुरुषोत्तमयोगः
śrīmadbhagavadgītā pañcadaśo'dhyāyaḥ - puruṣottamayogaḥ

Authors: Adarsh Saxena & Vijay Kumar

Identifiers

ISBN: 978-1-945739-51-4 (Paperback)
—o—

Coming Soon:
Gita Mūlaṁ 01 – Bhagavad Gita Chapter One
Gita Mūlaṁ 02 – Bhagavad Gita Chapter Two
Gita Mūlaṁ 03 – Bhagavad Gita Chapter Three
Gita Mūlaṁ 04 – Bhagavad Gita Chapter Four
Gita Mūlaṁ 05 – Bhagavad Gita Chapter Five (Available, ISBN: 978-1-945739-75-0)
Gita Mūlaṁ 06 – Bhagavad Gita Chapter Six
Gita Mūlaṁ 07 – Bhagavad Gita Chapter Seven
Gita Mūlaṁ 08 – Bhagavad Gita Chapter Eight
Gita Mūlaṁ 09 – Bhagavad Gita Chapter Nine
Gita Mūlaṁ 10 – Bhagavad Gita Chapter Ten
Gita Mūlaṁ 11 – Bhagavad Gita Chapter Eleven
Gita Mūlaṁ 12 – Bhagavad Gita Chapter Twelve (Available, ISBN: 978-1-945739-52-1)
Gita Mūlaṁ 13 – Bhagavad Gita Chapter Thirteen
Gita Mūlaṁ 14 – Bhagavad Gita Chapter Fourteen
Gita Mūlaṁ 15 – Bhagavad Gita Chapter Fifteen (Available, ISBN: 978-1-945739-51-4)
Gita Mūlaṁ 16 – Bhagavad Gita Chapter Sixteen (Available, ISBN: 978-1-945739-76-7)
Gita Mūlaṁ 17 – Bhagavad Gita Chapter Seventeen
Gita Mūlaṁ 18 – Bhagavad Gita Chapter Eighteen
[All 18 books in this Gita Mūlaṁ series (for each chapter of the Bhagavad-Gitā) will become available by December 2025]

—o—

Our Bhagavad-Gitā Books:
Bhagavad Gita, The Holy Book of Hindus, with Sanskrit Text, English Translation & Transliteration, No Commentary.
-ISBN: 978-1-945739-36-1 / 978-1-945739-37-8 (Paperback/Hardback. Book Size 6.14"x9.21"x190 pages)
-ISBN: 978-1-945739-39-2 (For Gitā Journaling. 8"x8"x390 pages)
-ISBN: 978-1-945739-43-9 (Convenient Pocket-Sized Edition. 4"x6"x180 pages)
-ISBN: 978-1-945739-40-8 (Legacy Book. 7.5"x9.25"x246 pages)
-ISBN: 978-1-945739-55-2 / 978-1-945739-56-9 (Paperback/Hardback. For Note-Taking. 7.5"x9.25"x190 pages)

Also Available:
- **Tulsi Ramayana—Hindu Holy Book:** Ramcharitmanas with English Translation (ISBNs: 978-1-945739-**60-6**, 978-1-945739-**61-3**)
- **Ramcharitmanas - Large/Medium/Small** (No Translation)
- **Sundarakanda:** The Fifth-Ascent of Tulsi Ramayana (ISBNs: 978-1-945739-**05-7**, 978-1-945739-**15-6**)
- **Rama Hymns:** Hanuman-Chalisa, Rāma-Raksha-Stotra, etc. (ISBNs: 978-1-945739-**25-5**, 978-1-945739-**09-5**)
- **Vivekachudamani, Fiery Crest-Jewel of Wisdom** (ISBNs: 978-1-945739-**44-6**, 978-1-945739-**45-3**, 978-1-945739-**41-5**)
- **Ashtavakra Gītā, the Fiery Octave** (ISBNs: 978-1-945739-**46-0**, 978-1-945739-**47-7**, 978-1-945739-**42-2**)
- **Legacy Books - Endowment of Devotion (several):** Journal Books of sacred Hindu Hymns around which the Holy-Name Rama Name can be written; available in Paperback and Hardcover for: **Hanuman Chalisa** (ISBN: 1945739274/ 1945739940) **Sundara-Kanda** (ISBN: 1945739908/ 1945739916) **Rama-Raksha-Stotra** (ISBN: 1945739991/ 1945739967) **Bhushundi-Ramayana** (ISBN: 1945739983/ 1945739975) **Nama-Ramayanam** (ISBN: 1945739304/ 1945739959)
- **Rama Jayam - Likhita Japam Rama-Nama Mala alongside Sacred Hindu Texts (several):** Books for writing the 'Rama' Name 100,000 Times. Rama Jayam - Likhita Japam:Rama-Nama Mala. Available in Book Size 8"x10" (Paperback) for: **Hanuman Chalisa** (ISBN: 1945739169) **Rama Raksha Stotra** (ISBN: 1945739185) **Nama-Ramayanam** (ISBN: 1945739045) **Ramashtakam** (ISBN: 1945739177) **Rama Shatanama Stotra** (ISBN: 1945739266) **Rama-Shatnamavalih** (ISBN: 1945739134) **Simple (I)** (ISBN: 1945739142)
- **Likhita Japam** - Paperback books for writing the 'Rama' Name in dotted grids: **One-Lettered Rama Mantra**, Book Size 8"x10" (ISBN: 1945739312) **Two-Lettered Rama Mantra,** Book Size 8"x10" (ISBN: 1945739320) **Three-Lettered Rama Mantra,** Book Size 8"x10" (ISBN: 1945739339) **Four-Lettered Rama Mantra,** Book Size 8"x10" (ISBN: 1945739347) **Simple (II)** Book Size 7.5"x9.25" (ISBN: 1945739193) **Simple (III)** Book Size 8"x8" (ISBN: 1945739282) **Simple (IV)** Book Size 8.5"x8.5" (ISBN: 1945739878) **Simple (V)** Book Size 8.5"x11" (ISBN: 1945739924)

CONTENTS

गीता मूलं १५
gītā mūlaṁ 15
श्रीमद्भगवद्गीता पञ्चदशोऽध्यायः - पुरुषोत्तमयोगः
śrīmadbhagavadgītā pañcadaśo'dhyāyaḥ - puruṣottamayogaḥ

bhagavad-gītā

श्रीमद्भगवद्गीता

प्रथमोऽध्यायः - अर्जुनविषादयोगः

द्वितीयोऽध्यायः - साङ्ख्ययोगः

तृतीयोऽध्यायः - कर्मयोगः

चतुर्थोऽध्यायः - ज्ञानकर्मसंन्यासयोगः

पञ्चमोऽध्यायः - संन्यासयोगः

षष्ठोऽध्यायः - ध्यानयोगः

सप्तमोऽध्यायः - ज्ञानविज्ञानयोगः

अष्टमोऽध्यायः - अक्षरब्रह्मयोगः

नवमोऽध्यायः - राजविद्याराजगुह्ययोगः

दशमोऽध्यायः - विभूतियोगः

एकादशोऽध्यायः - विश्वरूपदर्शनयोगः

द्वादशोऽध्यायः - भक्तियोगः

त्रयोदशोऽध्यायः - क्षेत्रक्षेत्रज्ञविभागयोगः

चतुर्दशोऽध्यायः - गुणत्रयविभागयोगः

पञ्चदशोऽध्यायः - पुरुषोत्तमयोगः

षोडशोऽध्यायः - दैवासुरसम्पद्विभागयोगः

सप्तदशोऽध्यायः - श्रद्धात्रयविभागयोगः

अष्टादशोऽध्यायः - मोक्षसंन्यासयोगः

ॐ ॐ ॐ ॐ ॐ ॐ ॐ ॐ ॐ ॐ ॐ ॐ ॐ ॐ ॐ ॐ ॐ ॐ

— ॐ — ध्यानम् — ॐ — dhyānam — ॐ —

— ॐ — ॐ — ॐ — ॐ — ॐ — ॐ —

ॐ INVOCATIONS

ॐ श्री परमात्मने नमः

— om śrī paramātmane namaḥ —

[Om—I bow down to the Supreme-Energy, Supreme-Being]

त्वमेव माता च पिता त्वमेव । त्वमेव बंधुश्च सखा त्वमेव ।
tvameva mātā ca pitā tvameva , tvameva baṁdhuśca sakhā tvameva ,
त्वमेव विद्या द्रविणं त्वमेव । त्वमेव सर्वं मम देवदेव ॥
tvameva vidyā draviṇaṁ tvameva , tvameva sarvaṁ mama devadeva .

Thou art my mother and my father, Thou alone my kin, kith, friend; Thou alone my wisdom, knowledge, wealth; Thou alone—O God of gods—my all, and everything!

— ॐ —

शान्ताकारं भुजगशयनं पद्मनाभं सुरेशं । विश्वाधारं गगनसदृशं मेघवर्णं शुभाङ्गम् ।
śāntākāraṁ bhujagaśayanaṁ padmanābhaṁ sureśaṁ
viśvādhāraṁ gaganasadṛśaṁ meghavarṇaṁ śubhāṅgam ,
लक्ष्मीकान्तं कमलनयनं योगिभिर्ध्यानगम्यं । वन्दे विष्णुं भवभयहरं सर्वलोकैकनाथम् ॥
lakṣmīkāntaṁ kamalanayanaṁ yogibhirdhyānagamyaṁ
vande viṣṇuṁ bhavabhayaharaṁ sarvalokaikanātham .

I venerate Shri Vishnu—of a serene appearance who slumbers upon the serpent *Shesha-Nāga*, from whose navel has sprung the lotus of creation, who presides over as the God of gods, who is the substratum of the universe, boundless and infinite like the sky. Of a dark hue like the clouds, of a form radiating everlasting auspiciousness, with eyes beautiful like lotus petals, who is the beloved of Devī Lakshmī, who is reachable only through devotional meditation by Yogīs, who removes all fears of worldly existence—upon Him, Vishnu, the One Great Lord of all the worlds, I meditate.

— ॐ —

यं ब्रह्मा वरुणेन्द्ररुद्रमरुतः स्तुन्वन्ति दिव्यैः स्तवैः
yaṁ brahmā varuṇendrarudramarutaḥ stunvanti divyaiḥ stavaiḥ
वेदैः साङ्गपदक्रमोपनिषदैर्गायन्ति यं सामगाः ।
vedaiḥ sāṅgapadakramopaniṣadairgāyanti yaṁ sāmagāḥ ,
ध्यानावस्थिततद्गतेन मनसा पश्यन्ति यं योगिनो
dhyānāvasthitatadgatena manasā paśyanti yaṁ yogino
यस्यान्तं न विदुः सुरासुरगणा देवाय तस्मै नमः ॥
yasyāntaṁ na viduḥ surāsuragaṇā devāya tasmai namaḥ .

Unto That Supreme—whom Brahammā, Varuna, Indra, Rudra and the Mārutas praise with excellent holy hymns; who is versified throughout the Vedas and Upanishads by the chanters of Sāma; who—in perfect meditations deep—the yogis see within their own minds while absorbed in "That-One"; whose beginning and end, even gods and demi-gods never know of—unto That Supreme-Being, I offer my many venerations.

—ॐ— स्तुतिः —ॐ— stutiḥ —ॐ—

—ॐ—ॐ—ॐ—ॐ—ॐ—ॐ—

VENERATIONS

—ॐ—

पार्थाय प्रतिबोधितां भगवता नारायणेन स्वयम्
pārthāya pratibodhitāṁ bhagavatā nārāyaṇena svayam
व्यासेनग्रथितां पुराणमुनिना मध्ये महाभारते ।
vyāsenagrathitāṁ purāṇamuninā madhye mahābhārate ,
अद्वैतामृतवर्षिणीं भगवतीमष्टादशाध्यायिनीम्
advaitāmṛtavarṣiṇīṁ bhagavatīmaṣṭādaśādhyāyinīm
अम्ब त्वामनुसन्दधामि भगवद्गीते भवेद्वेषिणीम् ॥
amba tvāmanusandadhāmi bhagavadgīte bhavedveṣiṇīm .

O Thou Bhagavad-Gītā—with whom Pārtha was enlightened by the Lord Nārāyana himself; who was integrated into the Mahābhārata by the ancient sage Vyāsa; O Thou blessed Mother—who with her eighteen Cantos shower humanity with the nectar of Advaita; O Thou destroyer of rebirths, upon Thee—O Bhagavad-Gītā, O loving Mother—I meditate.

—ॐ—

नमोऽस्तु ते व्यास विशालबुद्धे फुल्लारविन्दायतपत्रनेत्र ।
namo'stu te vyāsa viśālabuddhe phullāravindāyatapatranetra ,
येन त्वया भारततैलपूर्णः प्रज्वालितो ज्ञानमयः प्रदीपः ॥
yena tvayā bhāratatailapūrṇaḥ prajvālito jñānamayaḥ pradīpaḥ .

Salutations to Thee O Vyāsa—of a mighty intellect and with eyes large like the petals of a full-blossomed lotus; by whom has been forever lit in this world the Lamp-of-Wisdom, filled with the oil in the form of the great epic: Mahābhārata.

— ॐ —

प्रपन्नपारिजाताय तोत्रवेत्रैकपाणये ।
prapannapārijātāya totravetraikapāṇaye ,
ज्ञानमुद्राय कृष्णाय गीतामृतदुहे नमः ॥
jñānamudrāya kṛṣṇāya gītāmṛtaduhe namaḥ .

He—who is the wish-granting tree of the suppliant—in whose one hand is held the rope for cow and with the other hand who holds the Yogic posture of *Jnana*—who is the milcher of the nectar known as Gītā—unto Him, Krishna, my repeated venerations.

— ॐ —

सर्वोपनिषदो गावो दोग्धा गोपालनन्दनः ।
sarvopaniṣado gāvo dogdhā gopālanandanaḥ ,
पार्थो वत्सः सुधीर्भोक्ता दुग्धं गीतामृतं महत् ॥
pārtho vatsaḥ sudhīrbhoktā dugdhaṁ gītāmṛtaṁ mahat .

All the Upanishads are the cows; the milcher is the joy of cowherds, Krishna; Pārtha is the calf; the man of purified understanding is the partaker; and the milk is verily the supreme nectar known as Gītā.

— ॐ —

वसुदेवसुतं देवं कंसचाणूरमर्दनम् ।
vasudevasutaṁ devaṁ kaṁsacāṇūramardanam ,
देवकीपरमानन्दं कृष्णं वन्दे जगद्गुरुम् ॥
devakīparamānandaṁ kṛṣṇaṁ vande jagadgurum .

I worship the charioteer, the Lord-God, the destroyer of Kamsa and Chānura, the supreme joy of Devakī, the son of Vāsudeva—Shri Krishna, the Universal Guru.

— ॐ —

भीष्मद्रोणतटा जयद्रथजला गान्धारनीलोत्पला
bhīṣmadroṇataṭā jayadrathajalā gāndhāranīlotpalā
शल्यग्राहवती कृपेण वहनी कर्णेन वेलाकुला ।
śalyagrāhavatī kṛpeṇa vahanī karṇena velākulā ,
अश्वत्थामविकर्णघोरमकरा दुर्योधनावर्तिनी
aśvatthāmavikarṇaghoramakarā duryodhanāvartinī
सोत्तीर्णा खलु पाण्डवैरणनदी कैवर्तकः केशवः ॥
sottīrṇā khalu pāṇḍavairaṇanadī kaivartakaḥ keśavaḥ .

That terrible battle-river—which had Bhīṣma and Droṇa as its two banks, and Jayadrathaja as its waters; which had the king of Gāndhāra as its blue lotus, and Śalya as its shark; whose currents and billows were Kṛipā and Karṇa; which had Aśvatthāmā and Vikarṇa as its terrible alligators; and of which Duryodhana was the deadly whirlpool—that ferocious river could be forded by the Pāṇḍavas only because they had Keśava as their helmsman.

— ॐ —

पाराशर्यवचः सरोजममलं गीतार्थगन्धोत्कटं
pārāśaryavacaḥ sarojamamalaṁ gītārthagandhotkaṭaṁ
नानाख्यानककेसरं हरिकथासम्बोधनाबोधितम्।
nānākhyānakakesaraṁ harikathāsambodhanābodhitam ।
लोके सज्जनषट्पदैरहरहः पेपीयमानं मुदा
loke sajjanaṣaṭpadairaharahaḥ pepīyamānaṁ mudā
भूयाद्भारतपङ्कजं कलिमलप्रध्वंसिनः श्रेयसे ॥
bhūyādbhāratapaṅkajaṁ kalimalapradhvaṁsinaḥ śreyase .

May this Lotus called Mahābhārata—which was born on the lake of the words of Vyāsa—which is perfumed with the fragrance of the Purport-of-Gītā—which has its innumerous stories as the pollen—which became fully bloomed through the discourses of Hari—which is the destroyer of the sins of the Kali-Yuga—which is everyday partaken joyously by the bees in the shape of good people of the world—may it bestow all goodness upon us.

— ॐ —

मूकं करोति वाचालं पङ्गुं लङ्घयते गिरिम् ।
mūkaṁ karoti vācālaṁ paṅguṁ laṅghayate girim ,
यत्कृपा तमहं वन्दे परमानन्दमाधवम् ॥
yatkṛpā tamahaṁ vande paramānandamādhavam .

I salute the Supreme-Being of the nature of supreme bliss, by whose very grace the dumb become eloquent and the cripples step across mountains.

— ॐ —

ॐ पूर्णमदः पूर्णमिदं पूर्णात् पूर्णमुदच्यते ।
om pūrṇamadaḥ pūrṇamidaṁ pūrṇāt pūrṇamudacyate ,
पूर्णस्य पूर्णमादाय पूर्णमेवावशिष्यते ।
pūrṇasya pūrṇamādāya pūrṇamevāvaśiṣyate ,
ॐ शान्तिः शान्तिः शान्तिः ॥
om śāntiḥ śāntiḥ śāntiḥ .

Om—That One (the unmanifest Brahma)—is infinite, complete, Entire; this (the manifest universe) is entire; And from That One fullness has emerged this entire universe here; And even when this entirety here is taken out of that One-Entire, It still abides complete in all Its entireness! Om, peace—let there be tranquility all around me!

— ॐ — ॐ — ॐ — ॐ — ॐ — ॐ — ॐ — ॐ — ॐ —

ॐ ॐ ॐ ॐ ॐ ॐ ॐ ॐ ॐ ॐ ॐ ॐ ॐ ॐ ॐ ॐ ॐ ॐ

ॐ The Journey Thus Far

— ॐ तत सत ॐ —

The *Bhagavad-Gītā* is a compendium of spiritual ideas on *Dharma* (righteous duty), *Bhakti* (devotion), *Karma* (action), *Moksha* (liberation), *Jnana* (knowledge), and *Yoga* (spiritual practice). Alongside the *Rāmāyana*, the *Gītā* is considered the most important Hindu scripture and counted among the classics of Indian spirituality. It is a collection of 700 verses culled from the *Bhīshma-Parva* of the epic *Mahābhārata*. Unlike the Vedas and Upanishads, scriptures like the *Mahābhārata* and *Rāmāyana* are historical records known as *Itihāsas*, which literally means 'Thus-happened...'—or history.

Set in the middle of the battlefield of Kurukshetra, the *Bhagavad-Gītā* unfolds as a profound dialogue between Arjuna, a warrior prince, and his charioteer, Bhagwāna Shri Krishna. This war, an epic clash involving vast armies from across the Āryavrata subcontinent, was surficially a family feud over the throne of Hastināpur between the Pandavas and the Kauravas—two branches of the same royal dynasty, but deeper down it is a battle between Dharma and Adharma.

As the battle is about to commence, we find Arjuna suddenly become overcome with deep moral confusion and despair at the violence and death which's about to be unleashed, and he starts to question the purpose and righteousness of the impending carnage. And at that pivotal poignant moment on the battlefield of Kurukshetra, when Arjuna—his heart heavy with sorrow and confusion—has sunk to his knees, unwilling and unable to fight, his sense of duty clouded and his purpose forgotten, Bhagwāna Shri Krishna speaks to Arjuna; and what follows is not merely a counsel unto a troubled warrior but a timeless discourse which has ever since shaped the moral and spiritual destinies of countless seekers in the battlefield of life.

Through the divine teachings of the Gitā, Bhagwāna Shri Krishna has revealed the eternal principles of duty, righteousness, and devotion—guiding humanity to self-realization, reminding each soul of his true identity—lighting the path to happiness and ultimate freedom: that of complete emancipation.

— ॐ —

A Brief Overview of the Chapters Leading up to Chapter 15

The entirety of Bhagavad-Gītā stands as an eternal beacon, lifting the human spirit beyond despair toward wisdom, purpose, and liberation; and today we stand at the threshold of chapter 15; here's a brief overview of what has transpired thus far:

In **Chapter 1** *(Arjuna Vishāda Yoga)*, we find the battlefield set and Arjuna struck by deep *vishāda* (despondency), overwhelmed by sorrow and moral crisis as he surveys his kin on both sides and drops his bow in despair.

At this point, in **Chapter 2** *(Sankhya Yoga)*, Krishna begins his spiritual teachings, reminding Arjuna of the immortality of the soul (Ātmā) and the importance of doing one's duty with detachment.

In **Chapter 3** *(Karma Yoga)*, Krishna elaborates on the path of Karma-Yoga, urging Arjuna to act for duties sake, without attachment to the results.

In **Chapter 4** *(Jnana-Karma-Sannyāsa Yoga)*, Krishna explains the higher knowledge that purifies karma, and He discusses the nature of divine incarnations.

In **Chapter 5**, the *Yoga of Renunciation*, Krishna reconciles the paths of renunciation and action, teaching that both can lead to liberation if performed with the right understanding.

Chapters 6 to 11 cover deeper insights into meditation, the balanced mind, and Krishna's revelation of his cosmic form *(Vishwarupa)*, giving Arjuna a vision of the universal divine presence.

Chapters 12 to 14 focus on the paths of devotion *(Bhakti Yoga)*, the qualities of true devotees, and a detailed explanation of the three *Gunas* (modes of nature) that shape human behaviour and bondage.

And now we find ourselves at **Chapter 15**, where Bhagwāna Shri Krishna will teach Arjuna about the *Purushottama Yoga*—the Yoga of the Supreme-Being.

This chapter presents a powerful allegory of the cosmic Ashvattha tree, symbolizing the inverted and entangling nature of material existence. Shri Krishna describes how one must cut down this deluding tree with the sword of detachment and seek refuge in the Supreme-Being *(Purushottama)*, who transcends both the perishable world and the imperishable soul. The chapter beautifully bridges metaphysical understanding with devotional realization, guiding us toward the highest goal: the emancipation of the self.

ॐ CHAPTER FIFTEEN, A BIRD'S-EYE VIEW

— ॐ तत सत ॐ —

PURUSHOTTAMA YOGA

Having traversed the profound teachings of *prakriti* (nature), *purusha* (the soul), and the interplay of the three *gunas* in preceding chapters, we have arrived at a crucial juncture in the *Bhagavad Gītā*. Chapter 15 stands as a luminous summit, distilling the essence of the *Gītā's* wisdom into a concise yet lofty meditation on the nature of existence and the supreme Reality that transcends everything.

Chapter 15 stands situated quite near to the closing stages of Krishna's discourse to Arjuna—which of course go on until chapter 18, and here Bhagwāna Shri Krishna seeks to elevate Arjuna's understanding beyond mere intellectual analysis and moral exhortation—guiding him instead toward the direct vision of the Supreme Being *(Purushottama)*.

Having revealed in the earlier chapters about the cyclical nature of birth and death, the dynamics of matter and spirit and the means to rise above them, Shri Krishna now unveils the highest metaphysical truth: the reality of the *Purushottama*—the Supreme-Being who stands above both the mutable world and the immutable soul.

— ॐ —

A QUICK TOUR

Chapter 15 unfolds in a precise and methodical manner. It opens with a striking cosmic allegory—the upside-down *ashvattha* tree—illustrating the entangling nature of existence.

Krishna then charts the soul's journey through endless embodiments, and He hints that it is He Himself, the Supreme-One, who went on to become the individual soul—and as which He is now sporting as the jiva in the world; and further indicates how it is He indeed who pervades all of creation; and then Krishna goes on to enumerate the distinction between perishable matter, the imperishable soul, and the Supreme-Being *Purushottama* —which of course too is Krishna.

Indeed Bhagwāna Shri Krishna is the formless ocean of existence-bliss-consciousness satt-chitt-ānanda braham, and who also exists in His manifest form as Krishna.

The chapter culminates in the crowning revelation that knowing the *Purushottama* leads to the highest wisdom and spiritual fulfilment.

— ॐ —

Now let us quickly skim verse by verse through the sacred terrain of Chapter 15.

- In verse 1, Krishna begins with the parable of the *ashvattha* tree, whose roots are upwards and branches down, symbolizing the entangled universe sustained by the Supreme.
- In verse 2, He describes how the branches of this cosmic tree extend due to the *gunas*, and its shoots are the objects of sense-enjoyment, entangling the soul.
- In verse 3, the Lord declares that this world-tree cannot be fully understood in its present form and must be cut down by the strong axe of detachment.
- In verse 4, we are urged to seek that supreme abode from which none return, placing our full faith in the Primeval-Being.
- *In verse 5, Krishna tells us that only the undeluded—those free of pride, attachment, and dualities—can attain the eternal goal.*
- In verse 6, Krishna reveals that His supreme abode, the *parama dhama*, is illuminated neither by sun nor moon, and reaching it, one never returns to this mortal plane.
- In verse 7, the nature of the individual soul is explained: an eternal portion of the Lord that, due to association with matter, struggles with the senses.
- In verse 8, Krishna illustrates the soul's journey from body to body, carrying with it the subtle senses, like the wind carrying away the scent.
- In verse 9, He describes how the soul experiences objects through the senses, whether in a body or after departing from it.
- **In verse 10, He notes that the ignorant do not perceive the soul's departure or experience, but the wise see that with clarity.**
- *In verse 11, Krishna explains that seekers with yogic vision behold the soul, while the unrefined and unintelligent fail to see it, even when taught.*
- In verse 12, He reveals that the light of the sun, moon, and fire all emanate from His brilliance—which sustains all life.
- *In verse 13, He declares that pervading the earth, it is He, Bhagwāna Shri Krishna, who upholds all beings and nourishes all vegetation through the sap of vitality.*

- In verse 14, Krishna proclaims that He is the digestive fire in all beings, aiding in the assimilation of food.
- In verse 15, He affirms that He resides in the hearts of all, and that from Him arise memory, knowledge, and their absence; He is the essence of all the Vedas.
- In verse 16, Bhagwāna Shri Krishna introduces the two types of beingness: the perishable (*kshara*) and the imperishable (*akshara*) that pervade through existence.
- In verse 17, Krishna declares the *uttama purusha*—the Supreme-Being—as distinct and transcendent, sustaining and permeating all.
- In verse 18, He asserts that because He is beyond both the perishable and the imperishable, He is rightly celebrated in the Vedas and the world as the Purushottama, the Supreme-One.
- In verse 19, Krishna promises that whoever, undeludedly, knows Him as the Supreme-Being, attains full wisdom and perforce worships Him wholeheartedly.
- In verse 20, Krishna concludes by declaring this doctrine to be the most esoteric of all teachings. Knowing it, the seeker attains true wisdom and fulfills the ultimate purpose of life.

Chapter 15 spans a majestic course: from the roots of cosmic entanglement to the heights of supreme realization. It prepares us for the next unfolding in Chapter 16, where Bhagwāna Shri Krishna will turn His gaze toward the ethical and psychological realms, distinguishing between the divine and the demoniacal *(daivī* and *āsurī)*, guiding us further on how to cultivate the virtues which lead to emancipation.

— ॐ लोकनाथाय नमः ॐ —

Lo, The Fifteenth Flame Arises

Among the lamps of Gita's scroll, one flame brilliantly shines:
the Fifteenth-Canto bright—which pierces the worldly dream with its fiery Light.
No cry of war heard herein, no chariot-wheels resound—
But hush descends -- and roots of Truth emerge from holy ground.
A Tree is drawn—with roots aloft and branches cast below,
It mirrors all we mortals see, yet hides the Truth which only the Wise know.
This is no Tree of fruitful grace—but lovely facade of quivering veils,
And they who are wise—arise with a shining sword,
To cut down this tangling tree—and ascend away to Freedom's skies.
O behold this Fifteenth—Jewel of thought such pure and deep—
Which is reckoned to be the Gita's very own heart.

ॐ ॐ ॐ ॐ ॐ ॐ ॐ ॐ ॐ ॐ ॐ ॐ ॐ ॐ ॐ ॐ ॐ ॐ

पञ्चदशोऽध्यायः - पुरुषोत्तमयोगः
pañcadaśo'dhyāyaḥ - puruṣottamayogaḥ
:: Canto – XV ::
- Path to the Supreme God-Head -

ॐ ॐ ॐ ॐ ॐ ॐ ॐ ॐ ॐ ॐ ॐ ॐ ॐ ॐ ॐ ॐ ॐ ॐ

ॐ गीता श्लोकः १५.१ – GĪTĀ VERSE 15.1

ॐ श्रीमद्भगवद्गीतासूपनिषत्सु ब्रह्मविद्यायां योगशास्त्रे श्रीकृष्णार्जुनसंवादे
om śrīmadbhagavadgītāsūpaniṣatsu brahmavidyāyāṁ yogaśāstre śrīkṛṣṇārjunasaṁvāde
पुरुषोत्तमयोगो नाम पञ्चदशोऽध्यायः श्लोकः १
puruṣottamayogo nāma pañcadaśo'dhyāyaḥ ślokaḥ 1

श्रीभगवानुवाच --
śrībhagavānuvāca --

ऊर्ध्वमूलमधःशाखमश्वत्थं प्राहुरव्ययम् ।
ūrdhvamūlamadhaḥśākhamaśvatthaṁ prāhuravyayam
छन्दांसि यस्य पर्णानि यस्तं वेद स वेदवित् ॥ १५-१ ॥
chandāṁsi yasya parṇāni yastaṁ veda sa vedavit (15-1)

***Shri Bhagwāna said:* "They speak of an immutable *Ashvattha* Tree—with its roots above, and its branches below, and which has the Vedas for its leaves—and he who knows it is the knower of the Vedas.** (15.1)

—: Word-by-Word :—

श्रीभगवानुवाच śrībhagavān uvāca – the Blessed Lord said; ऊर्ध्वमूलम् ūrdhva-mūlam – with roots upward; अधःशाखम् adhaḥ-śākham – branches downward; अश्वत्थम् aśvattham – the sacred fig tree (symbolic of the material world); प्राहुः prāhuḥ – they say; अव्ययम् avyayam – imperishable; छन्दांसि chandāṁsi – the Vedic hymns; यस्य yasya – whose; पर्णानि parṇāni – leaves; यः yaḥ – who; तम् tam – that; वेद veda – knows; सः saḥ – he; वेदवित् veda-vit – knower of the Vedas.

—: Understanding The Verse :—

— श्रीकृष्णाय नमः —

The fifteenth chapter of the Bhagavad-Gītā opens with an image of profound subtlety and grandeur, an image that has captivated seekers and philosophers across the ages. Here, the Lord begins to unveil the mystery of existence through the allegory of the cosmic अश्वत्था Ashvattha tree.

The unique configuration of this tree symbolizes the Supreme Being ऊर्ध्वमूलम् (Urdhvamūla) as the origin and sustainer of all existence.

The मूल mūla, or root, represents the eternal foundation—Paramātman—while the descending branches अधःशाखम् (Adhaḥśākham) denote the created universe, from Brahammā down to the minutest creatures. God, being transcendent, is the source of all creation and the sustainer of Dharma.

— ॐ श्रीरामाय नमः ॐ —

Though we, as individual souls, are verily a spark of the Supreme, a fragment of that eternal, conscious bliss—सच्चिदानन्द ब्रह्म Sat-Chit-Ānanda Braham—we, in our forgetfulness, cleave not to our divinity, but instead bind ourselves to the mutable and perishable: to the body, the senses, the mind, and the intellect; and although seen springing forth from the same Divine, these are but mere shadows of the undying underlying Reality, the Ātmā, which's far closer to our Self.

By mistaking this manifest world to be the ultimate, and by ascribing to it the notions of 'I,' 'me', 'mine,' 'for me,' through that 'moha', alas we become more and more entangled in the intricate snares of संसार saṁsāra, and thus we keep revolving in the endless cycle of births and deaths.

It is this illusory world-tree—this vast, tangled undergrowth of worldly existence—which forms the principal obstacle to realizing our true nature. And here Bhagwāna Shri Krishna is teaching us exactly of that.

—: *Key Sanskrit Terms* :—

In compassionate wisdom, the Lord, in these opening verses, sets forth a vivid depiction of the universe as a mighty पीपल वृक्ष Peepul tree, inverted in its growth, and would later on instruct the aspirant to sever its binding hold with the sharp axe of detachment.

Now let us unfold the inner meaning of this beautiful verse—that has been guiding souls from bondage toward supreme liberation over the generations—through an analysis of the verse's key Sanskrit terms:

— ॐ —

श्रीभगवानुवाच (shribhagavānuvācha) – "The Blessed Lord said":

This solemn invocation, recurrent throughout the Gītā, reminds us that the wisdom imparted is not merely human deliberation but a divine instruction. It is Bhagwāna-Shri, the Supreme Being—He who is complete with Shri -- beauty, majesty, and auspiciousness—who is speaking to us.

— ॐ —

ऊर्ध्वमूलमधःशाखम् (ūrdhvamūlam-adhaḥśākham) – "With roots above and branches below":

O how poetic; and not merely poetic but this inversion is spot-on and deeply symbolic. The ऊर्ध्वमूलम् ūrdhva-mūla points to the Supreme Source—पर-ब्रह्म Para-Braham—from whom this entire existence has egressed.

अधःशाखम् Adhaḥ-śākham signifies the descent of multiplicity from a Oneness—the diversified expressions of manifold existence in the world below. It subtly reflects the hierarchy of being, from the One to the seeming many.

— ॐ —

अश्वत्थम् (ashvattham) – "The sacred fig tree (peepul)":

Rich in symbolic meaning, the ashvattha is said to be impermanent अ-श्व-थ (a-śva-tha: "not the same tomorrow"), even though it is said to be eternal. Its ever-changing nature points toward the transitory realm, संसार saṁsāra, which only the ignorant perceive as permanent. And yet here, paradoxically it is being called अव्ययम् avyayam, a term we will talk of next.

— ॐ —

प्राहुः अव्ययम् (prāhuḥ avyayam) – "Declared to be immutable":

A paradox arises. The tree, emblematic of the mutable world—ever fluxing, ever changing, ever perishing, dying and then being reborn—is still termed avyayam अव्ययम् —imperishable!

Well, this reflects how the phenomenal world appears enduring due to Māyā माया. The illusion of continuity veils its underlying impermanence. It is avyayam अव्ययम् only in the sense that the cycle of birth and death, creation and dissolution, is unending until liberation dawns.

Births and deaths are but change of forms. Our real release is when we go beyond being just these fluxing wave and simply submerse back in the ocean—into the state of wavelessness.

— ॐ —

छन्दांसि (chandāṁsi) – "The Vedas":

छन्द Chandas refers to the metrical hymns of the Veda, and metaphorically, they form the पर्णानि parṇāni—leaves of the tree. Leaves nourish and protect the tree, just as Vedic knowledge upholds dharma and guides beings through the maze of karma and jnāna.

— ॐ —

यस्तं वेद स वेदवित् (yastaṁ veda sa vedavit) – "He who knows this, knows the Vedas":

Here, वेद veda is used both as scriptural knowledge (the ritualistic part) and as true knowing (of the essence of existence).

To grasp the essence of this अश्वत्थ ashvattha is to comprehend the heart of Vedic wisdom—namely, the transient nature of worldly life and the pathway beyond it – to the formless One.

—: *In Brief* :—

— ॐ श्रीकृष्णाय नमः ॐ —

This beautiful Verse 15.1 offers a profound, layered understanding of the world and our place within it. The imagery of the tree with its root in the unmanifest and its branches in the manifest highlights the connection between the eternal, changeless reality (Braham) and the ephemeral, illusory experience of life.

This verse serves as a call to see beyond the branches and leaves of the material world, to seek the very origin of everything—as abiding rooted within ब्रह्म Braham: who is the non-dual Reality beyond time, beyond names and shapes.

— ॐ श्रीरामाय नमः ॐ —

This wondrous tree is declared to be peculiar, for it stands with its roots above—rooted in the supreme realm of Braham, the unmanifest essence—and its branches spread below, reaching into the manifold planes of worldly existence.

This inversion itself reveals a truth: That all which is seen and experienced flows forth from that higher reality, drawing its sustenance and being from an eternal source.

— ॐ प्रद्युम्नाय नमः ॐ —

Just as every sprout, leaf, and tendril of a tree is nourished by its unseen roots, so too does this universe in all its vastness. This cosmos full of forms emanate from and depend upon Braham for its very existence and continuity.

This cosmic tree, with the Vedas as its leaves—signifying both nourishment and the means of knowledge —exists solely by dint of that divine substratum.

Remember: recognizing the structure alone is not the culmination; the true knower is he who sees through this illusory expanse to its very eternal foundation. With this vision, the Lord later on prepares to guide we seekers toward the next vital step: the method of severance by which the jīva, by cutting through the bonds of illusion, can ascend toward the imperishable goal: emancipation from this entangling world.

— ॐ तत सत ॐ —

Before we move on, let us bow in reverence to this sacred verse—a timeless beacon of wisdom guiding seekers for ages. Write it by hand, reflect on its meaning, and chant it aloud, for these sounds alone carry the authenticity of that era. The world may have changed but the living vibration of these Sanskrit sounds still remain as original as they were when Bhagwān Shri Krishna Himself walked the earth and imparted these teachings.

— ॐ —

श्रीभगवानुवाच --
śrībhagavānuvāca --
ऊर्ध्वमूलमधःशाखमश्वत्थं प्राहुरव्ययम् ।
ūrdhvamūlamadhaḥśākhamaśvatthaṁ prāhuravyayam
छन्दांसि यस्य पर्णानि यस्तं वेद स वेदवित् ॥ १५-१ ॥
chandāṁsi yasya parṇāni yastaṁ veda sa vedavit (15-1)

— ॐ —
श्रीभगवानुवाच -- śrībhagavānuvāca
ऊर्ध्वमूलमधःशाखमश्वत्थं प्राहुरव्ययम् ।
ūrdhvamūlamadhaḥśākhamaśvatthaṁ prāhuravyayam
छन्दांसि यस्य पर्णानि यस्तं वेद स वेदवित् ॥ १५-१ ॥
chandāṁsi yasya parṇāni yastaṁ veda sa vedavit (15-1)

ॐ तत्सदिति श्रीमद्भगवद्गीतासूपनिषत्सु ब्रह्मविद्यायां योगशास्त्रे श्रीकृष्णार्जुनसंवादे
om tatsaditi śrīmadbhagavadgītāsūpaniṣatsu brahmavidyāyāṁ yogaśāstre śrīkṛṣṇārjunasaṁvāde
पुरुषोत्तमयोगो नाम पञ्चदशोऽध्यायः श्लोकः १
puruṣottamayogo nāma pañcadaśo'dhyāyaḥ ślokaḥ 1

Om-Tat-Sat—Om (Braham) is the sole Reality. In the Yogic Scripture on the Science-of-Braham, the Shrimada-Bhāgvada-Gītā Upanishad, we hereby conclude Shloka 1 of the Dialogue between Shrī Krishna and Arjuna entitled Purushottama-Yoga, Canto XV.

ॐ गीता श्लोकः १५.२ – GĪTĀ VERSE 15.2

ॐ श्रीमद्भगवद्गीतासूपनिषत्सु ब्रह्मविद्यायां योगशास्त्रे श्रीकृष्णार्जुनसंवादे
om śrīmadbhagavadgītāsūpaniṣatsu brahmavidyāyāṁ yogaśāstre śrīkṛṣṇārjunasaṁvāde
पुरुषोत्तमयोगो नाम पञ्चदशोऽध्यायः श्लोकः २
puruṣottamayogo nāma pañcadaśo'dhyāyaḥ ślokaḥ 2

— ॐ —

अधश्चोर्ध्वं प्रसृतास्तस्य शाखा गुणप्रवृद्धा विषयप्रवालाः ।
adhaścordhvaṁ prasṛtāstasya śākhā guṇapravṛddhā viṣayapravālāḥ
अधश्च मूलान्यनुसन्ततानि कर्मानुबन्धीनि मनुष्यलोके ॥ १५-२ ॥
adhaśca mūlānyanusantatāni karmānubandhīni manuṣyaloke (15-2)

Its branches, nurtured by the *Gunas*, are spread above, around, below; and its shoots are the sense-objects; and its roots hang downwards—which are the producers of actions in this world of beings. (15.2)

—: *Word-by-Word* :—

अधः adhaḥ – downward; च ca – and; ऊर्ध्वम् ūrdhvam – upward; प्रसृताः prasṛtāḥ – spread out; तस्य tasya – its; शाखाः śākhāḥ – branches; गुणप्रवृद्धाः guṇa-pravṛddhāḥ – nourished by the modes (gunas); विषयप्रवालाः viṣaya-pravālāḥ – having sense objects as sprouts; अधः adhaḥ – downward; च ca – and; मूलानि mūlāni – roots; अनुसन्ततानि anusantatāni – extending; कर्मानुबन्धीनि karma-anubandhīni – bound by actions; मनुष्यलोके manuṣya-loke – in the world of humans.

—: *Understanding The Verse* :—

— ॐ श्रीकृष्णाय नमः ॐ —

Having introduced this inverted tree of existence in the previous verse, Bhagwāna Shri Krishna now turns our gaze toward its manifold branches and roots, offering a more vivid portrayal of the universe's unfolding. The Blessed Lord deepens His exposition of the cosmic Ashvattha tree, illuminating its intricate expanse and the forces which animate its gargantuan form.

This tree, a grand metaphor for the created world, is shown by Shri Krishna in all its complexity, with its branches—nurtured and shaped by the threefold गुण Gunas—extending above, below, and all around, signifying the countless realms and states of existence.

— ॐ श्रीरामाय नमः ॐ —

The Lord reveals that the sense-objects are like the tender offshoots which entice the soul outward into varied worldly experiences and the ensuing attachments and repulsions that become the cause of jīva's bondages.

Meanwhile, the tree's roots—which although inverted and having their source in the imperishable Braham—descend and embed themselves deep into the world of action, sustaining the ceaseless cycle of karma and rebirth.

Through this powerful image, the Lord unveils the intricate mesh of causations and desires that bind the individual soul to the wheel of संसार Saṁsāra, bespeaking of the profound mystery of existence, where the eternal and the ephemeral stay intertwined.

—: *Key Sanskrit Terms* :—

Let us trace the golden threads of its meaning by lingering within the verse's luminous Sanskrit terms—each a doorway into deeper realms.

— ॐ —

अधश्चोर्ध्वं प्रसृताः (adhaścordhvaṁ prasṛtāḥ) – "Spread below and above":

The proliferation of branches both above and below conveys the unrestricted spread of worldly existence संसार (saṁsāra) which we see around us.

The dual direction signifies both celestial and terrestrial planes—svarga and mratyuloka—where beings take birth and perform actions. It is symbolic of the soul's entanglement across realms, subject to कर्मफल karma-phala.

— ॐ —

तस्य शाखाः (tasya śākhāḥ) – "Its branches":

The branches of this cosmic ashvattha tree represent the myriad streams of worldly experiences and the various entanglements ensuing thence—of desires, ambitions, affiliations, and karmic bonds. Each branch corresponds to a path shaped by one's past actions and tendencies संस्कार (saṁskāras).

— ॐ —

गुणप्रवृद्धाः (gunapravṛddhāḥ) – "Nourished by the Gunas":

The Gunas—सत्त्व राजस तमस sattva, rajas, and tamas—are the constituents of Prakriti, and their play sustains this tree.

प्रवृद्धाः Pravṛddhāḥ signifies how the शाखाः śākhāḥ expand and multiply when the Gunas flourish. Each being's experiences and dispositions are shaped by the predominance and permutation of the Gunas.

— ॐ —

विषयप्रवालाः (vishayapravālāḥ) – "With sense-objects as their tender shoots":

विषय Vishaya—objects of the senses—are here likened to प्रवालाः pravālāḥ, tender leaves or new growths. Just as new shoots attract with their freshness, the vishayas lure the जीव Jīva, drawing him further into attachment and desire. These are the entangling baits that bind the soul further deeper into संसार saṁsāra.

— ॐ —

अधश्च मूलानि अनुसन्ततानि (adhaśca mūlāni anusantatāni) – "And the roots stretch downward":

These downward-reaching roots symbolize actions (karma) and inclinations that bind the jīva to worldly life. While the primary foundational root is above—Braham who stays as the powerhouse sustaining the tree—the secondary roots descend into the lower realms, signifying entrenchment in the phenomenal.

— ॐ —

कर्मानुबन्धीनि (karmānubandhīni) – "Bound by action":

These roots are not passive; they are अनुबन्धीनि anubandhīni—they bind, connect, and tether the soul to the transmigrational cycle of birth and death. They are the causal links that hurl the जीव jīva into successive lifetimes born as the various creatures of the world.

— ॐ —

मनुष्यलोके (manuṣyaloke) – "In the human realm":

A human birth in the human world is uniquely emphasized, for here alone is the capacity for discernment विवेक (viveka) and liberation मोक्ष (moksha). It is within मनुष्य लोक manuṣya-loka that the Jīva can recognize his bondage and strive for release.

—: *In Brief* :—

— ॐ श्रीकृष्णाय नमः ॐ —

This second verse of Fifteenth reveals the grand tapestry of creation—woven through the power of the Gunas and which nourishes and sustains the manifold expressions of life.

The branches—symbolic of various planes of existence—spread in all directions, while the sense-objects, like alluring shoots, draw the living beings outward into the dance of desire and attachment.

The downward-hanging roots, ever busy in the soil of worldly action, perpetuate the cycle of birth and death, keeping the jīva enmeshed in the fabric of endless karmas.

Ah, how formidable and frightening this image! And yet we take comfort in that beneath all this ceaseless play lies the unchanging, divine substratum: the unseen root that alone gives life and coherence to the entire tree of the universe.

Discerning this truth is the key to breaking free from illusion.

— ॐ श्रीरामाय नमः ॐ —

In the next verse, Bhagwāna Shri Krishna discloses the very purpose behind this profound depiction of the cosmic tree, guiding us further towards the means of liberation from its binding grasp.

— ॐ तत सत ॐ —

Before we move on, let us bow in reverence to this sacred verse—a timeless beacon of wisdom guiding seekers for ages. Write it by hand, reflect on its meaning, and chant it aloud, for these sounds alone carry the authenticity of that era. The world may have changed but the living vibration of these Sanskrit sounds still remain as original as they were when Bhagwān Shri Krishna Himself walked the earth and imparted these teachings.

— ॐ —

अधश्चोर्ध्वं प्रसृतास्तस्य शाखा गुणप्रवृद्धा विषयप्रवालाः ।
adhaścordhvaṁ prasṛtāstasya śākhā guṇapravṛddhā viṣayapravālāḥ
अधश्च मूलान्यनुसन्ततानि कर्मानुबन्धीनि मनुष्यलोके ॥ १५-२ ॥
adhaśca mūlānyanusantatāni karmānubandhīni manuṣyaloke (15-2)

— ॐ —

अधश्चोर्ध्वं प्रसृतास्तस्य शाखा गुणप्रवृद्धा विषयप्रवालाः ।
adhaścordhvaṁ prasṛtāstasya śākhā guṇapravṛddhā viṣayapravālāḥ
अधश्च मूलान्यनुसन्ततानि कर्मानुबन्धीनि मनुष्यलोके ॥ १५-२ ॥
adhaśca mūlānyanusantatāni karmānubandhīni manuṣyaloke (15-2)

ॐ तत्सदिति श्रीमद्भगवद्गीतासूपनिषत्सु ब्रह्मविद्यायां योगशास्त्रे श्रीकृष्णार्जुनसंवादे
om tatsaditi śrīmadbhagavadgītāsūpaniṣatsu brahmavidyāyāṁ yogaśāstre śrīkṛṣṇārjunasaṁvāde
पुरुषोत्तमयोगो नाम पञ्चदशोऽध्यायः श्लोकः २
puruṣottamayogo nāma pañcadaśo'dhyāyaḥ ślokaḥ 2

Om-Tat-Sat—Om (Braham) is the sole Reality. In the Yogic Scripture on the Science-of-Braham, the Shrimada-Bhāgvada-Gītā Upanishad, we hereby conclude Shloka 2 of the Dialogue between Shrī Krishna and Arjuna entitled Purushottama-Yoga, Canto XV.

ॐ गीता श्लोकः १५.३ – GĪTĀ VERSE 15.3

ॐ श्रीमद्भगवद्गीतासूपनिषत्सु ब्रह्मविद्यायां योगशास्त्रे श्रीकृष्णार्जुनसंवादे
om śrīmadbhagavadgītāsūpaniṣatsu brahmavidyāyāṁ yogaśāstre śrīkṛṣṇārjunasaṁvāde
पुरुषोत्तमयोगो नाम पञ्चदशोऽध्यायः श्लोकः ३
puruṣottamayogo nāma pañcadaśo'dhyāyaḥ ślokaḥ 3

— ॐ —

न रूपमस्येह तथोपलभ्यते नान्तो न चादिर्न च सम्प्रतिष्ठा ।
na rūpamasyeha tathopalabhyate nānto na cādirna ca sampratiṣṭhā
अश्वत्थमेनं सुविरूढमूलं असङ्गशस्त्रेण दृढेन छित्त्वा ॥१५-३॥
aśvatthamenaṁ suvirūḍhamūlaṁ asaṅgaśastreṇa dṛḍhena chittvā (15-3)

This Tree of creation—in a continuous flux and lacking constancy of form—has no beginning or end. One should strive to shear away this deep rooted *Ashvattha* tree with the strong axe of dispassion. (15.3)

—: Word-by-Word :—

न na – not; रूपम् rūpam – form; अस्य asya – of this; इह iha – here; तथा tathā – in that way; उपलभ्यते upalabhyate – is perceived; न na – neither; अन्तः antaḥ – end; न च na ca – and nor; आदिः ādiḥ – beginning; न च na ca – and nor; सम्प्रतिष्ठा sampratiṣṭhā – foundation; अश्वत्थम् aśvattham – this sacred peepul tree; एनम् enam – this; सुविरूढमूलम् suvirūḍha-mūlam – well-rooted; असङ्गशस्त्रेण asaṅga-śastreṇa – with the weapon of detachment; दृढेन dṛḍhena – firm; छित्त्वा chittvā – having cut down.

—: Understanding The Verse :—

— ॐ श्रीकृष्णाय नमः ॐ —

Bhagwāna Shri Krishna has laid bare the form of the cosmic Ashvattha tree in the preceding two verses, and He now reveals a profound truth: that this tree—vast and all-pervading and which ultimately stays inscrutable to mortal vision—must be triumphed over. One should escape its snares—through Jnāna and dispassion.

This tree, a symbol of the tangled web of material existence, stands as a formidable barrier to our wellbeing and happiness; it's a roadblock on our path to emancipation. And although it is very formidable—and its true nature, its origin, its termination, and even its fundamental basis elude the grasp of those ensnared in worldly delusions—and yet we must endeavor to prevail over it by cutting it down ruthlessly through the sharp sword of dispassion.

— ॐ श्रीरामाय नमः ॐ —

Despite its detailed exposition, the essence of this tree cannot be fully comprehended through mere intellectual inquiry. The seeker is thus enjoined not to become entangled in endless speculation but rather to take decisive action forthwith—to sever away this deeply rooted Ashvattha with the mighty axe of वैराग्य Vairāgya (dispassion).

Bhagwāna Shri Krishna directs us toward the practical path of renunciation—pointing to the one sure means by which we may free ourselves from the binding coils of संसार Saṁsāra.

—: Key Sanskrit Terms :—

Let us draw back the veil of this verse, guided by the shimmering light of its key Sanskrit terms, each revealing unseen horizons.

— ॐ —

न रूपम् अस्येह तथोपलभ्यते (na rūpam asyeha tathopalabhyate) – "Its form is not perceived as is":

The word रूप rūpa denotes form or definable structure. Krishna declares that this cosmic ashvattha tree—symbolic of संसार saṁsāra—has no discernible or stable form in this इह (iha) world. It cannot be grasped through the senses or intellect in its totality.

None really can tell what is really out there.

All this visible is the veils of माया Māyā—which renders 'realness' to the formless; but that 'realness' stays fleeting and misleading.

— ॐ —

नान्तः न च आदिः न च सम्प्रतिष्ठा (nāntaḥ na ca ādiḥ na ca sampratiṣṭhā) – "It has neither end, nor beginning, nor stable foundation":

These three negations strike at the root of delusion. There is no beginning आदि (ādi) to this worldly manifestation, no end अन्त (anta) that can be perceived within the empirical realm, and no foundation सम्प्रतिष्ठा (sampratiṣṭhā)—no ultimate anchoring reality in the world of appearances. The verse echoes the illusory nature of the cosmic tree: that which seems vast and real lacks true ontological standing.

— ॐ —

अश्वत्थम् एनं सुविरूढमूलम् (ashvattham enaṁ suvirūḍhamūlam) – "This ashvattha, with its deeply entrenched roots":

The ashvattha of course stands for the world-tree. Here it is described as सुविरूढमूलम् suvirūḍhamūlam—having well-firmed secondary roots, indicating the strength and depth of the soul's bondage to worldly existence. These roots are karmic tendencies वासना (vāsanās), born of countless births, well established through attachment and identification with the non-Self.

— ॐ —

असङ्गशस्त्रेण दृढेन छित्त्वा (asaṅgaśastreṇa dṛḍhena chittvā) – "Having cut it down with the firm sword of non-attachment":

This is the verse's clarion call. The word असङ्ग asaṅga means non-attachment, dispassion, detachment from the fleeting. It is declared to be a शस्त्र shastra, a weapon like the sword.

Remember, not gentle persuasion, but a decisive severance is required.

And this शस्त्र shastra must be दृढ dṛḍha—unwavering, unshakable. Only by resolute वैराग्य vairāgya (detachment) can one cut the roots of संसार saṁsāra and begin the ascent to the Self.

—: In Brief :—

— ॐ श्रीरामाय नमः ॐ —

Above, around, and down it sways, this Tree without a start or end,
It casts no single, steadfast shade, Nor lifts us towards a skyward grace.
Its branches stretch through paths untrue;
where wandering souls, in folly, stray;
Each bough a snare of fleeting joy,
That lures the inner self away.
O mortal, beware of the fruits that stay sparkling bright here—
Look out: it is gleaming toxin that's laced upon these poisoned stems.

— o —

The gunas गुण tend these twinkling flames
With unseen hands and secret whims.
They stoke the fire of restless thought—that cling men to the things of earth.
O mind! This Tree thou climb'st so high—is not the path to lasting worth.
A wheel it is, in a savage spin—turning around, again and again,
With thee hanging hapless suspended—over a well of dark abyss.

— o —

O mortal, break free, awaken, seek the Root—
that blissful state—the Truth your brain missed—and your heart keeps missing.

— ॐ सत्यनन्दाय नमः ॐ —

This Ashvattha, the tree of cosmic existence, is declared to be beyond the ordinary grasp, for it cannot be discerned by those who remain immersed in worldly attachments.

Its beginning is veiled, its end is hidden, and its sustaining root remains unseen—such is the bewildering nature of Saṁsāra.

The deep secondary roots of this tree, entrenched in ignorance and desire, perpetuate the ceaseless cycle of birth and death.

— ॐ दूषण त्रिशिरो हन्त्रे नमः ॐ —

Though the task appears daunting, yet, the Lord assures us, this formidable tree, though ancient and widespread, is not invincible.

Armed with the resolute sword of dispassion and discernment, a sincere aspirant can very much cut through its entanglements and thereby set himself free from its bondage.

In the forthcoming verse, the Lord unfolds the next hallowed instruction: what we must simultaneously pursue while decisively severing away this tree.

— ॐ —

Before we move on, let us bow in reverence to this sacred verse. Write it by hand, reflect on its meaning, chant it aloud, make it your own.

— ॐ —

न रूपमस्येह तथोपलभ्यते नान्तो न चादिर्न च सम्प्रतिष्ठा ।
na rūpamasyeha tathopalabhyate nānto na cādirna ca sampratiṣṭhā
अश्वत्थमेनं सुविरूढमूलं असङ्गशस्त्रेण दृढेन छित्त्वा ॥१५-३॥
aśvatthamenaṁ suvirūḍhamūlaṁ asaṅgaśastreṇa dṛḍhena chittvā (15-3)

— ॐ —

न रूपमस्येह तथोपलभ्यते नान्तो न चादिर्न च सम्प्रतिष्ठा ।
na rūpamasyeha tathopalabhyate nānto na cādirna ca sampratiṣṭhā
अश्वत्थमेनं सुविरूढमूलं असङ्गशस्त्रेण दृढेन छित्त्वा ॥१५-३॥
aśvatthamenaṁ suvirūḍhamūlaṁ asaṅgaśastreṇa dṛḍhena chittvā (15-3)

ॐ तत्सदिति श्रीमद्भगवद्गीतासूपनिषत्सु ब्रह्मविद्यायां योगशास्त्रे श्रीकृष्णार्जुनसंवादे
om tatsaditi śrīmadbhagavadgītāsūpaniṣatsu brahmavidyāyāṁ yogaśāstre śrīkṛṣṇārjunasaṁvāde
पुरुषोत्तमयोगो नाम पञ्चदशोऽध्यायः श्लोकः ३
puruṣottamayogo nāma pañcadaśo'dhyāyaḥ ślokaḥ 3

Om-Tat-Sat—Om (Braham) is the sole Reality. In the Yogic Scripture on the Science-of-Braham, the Shrimada-Bhāgvada-Gītā Upanishad, we hereby conclude Shloka 3 of the Dialogue between Shrī Krishna and Arjuna entitled Purushottama-Yoga, Canto XV.

ॐ गीता श्लोकः १५.४ – GĪTĀ VERSE 15.4

ॐ श्रीमद्भगवद्गीतासूपनिषत्सु ब्रह्मविद्यायां योगशास्त्रे श्रीकृष्णार्जुनसंवादे
om śrīmadbhagavadgītāsūpaniṣatsu brahmavidyāyāṁ yogaśāstre śrīkṛṣṇārjunasaṁvāde
पुरुषोत्तमयोगो नाम पञ्चदशोऽध्यायः श्लोकः ४
puruṣottamayogo nāma pañcadaśo'dhyāyaḥ ślokaḥ 4

— ॐ —

ततः पदं तत्परिमार्गितव्यं यस्मिन्गता न निवर्तन्ति भूयः ।
tataḥ padaṁ tatparimārgitavyaṁ yasmingatā na nivartanti bhūyaḥ
तमेव चाद्यं पुरुषं प्रपद्ये यतः प्रवृत्तिः प्रसृता पुराणी ॥१५-४॥
tameva cādyaṁ puruṣaṁ prapadye yataḥ pravṛttiḥ prasṛtā purāṇī (15-4)

And thereafter one should diligently seek That supreme state—reaching which there is no return—by making a firm resolve: 'I take refuge in the primordial *Purusha* alone—from whom has sprung this eternal process, this great Tree of creation.' (15.4)

—: *Word-by-Word* :—

ततः tataḥ – then; पदम् padam – the state; तत् tat – that; परिमार्गितव्यम् parimārgitavyam – should be sought; यस्मिन् yasmin – in which; गताः gatāḥ – having gone; न निवर्तन्ति na nivartanti – do not return; भूयः bhūyaḥ – again; तम् tam – that; एव ca – indeed; आद्यम् ādyam – the original; पुरुषम् puruṣam – person (Supreme Being); प्रपद्ये prapadye – I surrender to; यतः yataḥ – from whom; प्रवृत्तिः pravṛttiḥ – the activity; प्रसृता prasṛtā – has extended; पुराणी purāṇī – ancient.

—: *Understanding The Verse* :—

— ॐ श्रीकृष्णाय नमः ॐ —

This verse stands as the luminous culmination of the profound allegory of the अश्वत्थ वृक्ष Ashvattha-vṛkṣa—the inverted world-tree that symbolizes the bewildering expanse of संसार saṁsāra—in which the jīva stays caught in an unremitting cycle of births, deaths, rebirths donning the bodies of various creatures of earth.

Having instructed the aspirant to sever the deep roots of attachment and karma with the sharp sword of असंग asaṅga (dispassion), the Blessed Lord now reveals the true aim: achieving oneness within the Supreme-Being.

Aye, that is the supreme quest which must follow renunciation: to gain oneness with Him.

— ॐ सदाहनुमदाश्रिताय नमः ॐ —

Indeed, this marks the true pivot from bondage to liberation.

Once the ties to the transient have been cut, the seeker is urged to turn unwaveringly toward the eternal essence—the आदि पुरुष Ādi-Purusha, the Primordial Being, from whom this timeless process of creation has sprung.

The aspirant, with steadfast resolve and one-pointed devotion, is enjoined to seek that supreme *pada* परम पद (abode), having attained which there is no return to the cycle of becoming.

Here, the Gītā lifts our vision from negation to the highest affirmation: from cutting down the illusory tree to embracing the immortal root of existence.

Trampling over the world with dispassion—not just for the heck of it but because this walking over forms is a requisite for reaching our real goal: gaining our oneness with the formless One.

—: *Key Sanskrit Terms* :—

Let us breathe with the verse's ancient cadence, allowing its vital Sanskrit terms to unfold their layered petals of meaning.

— ॐ —

ततः पदं तत् परिमार्गितव्यं (tataḥ padaṁ tat parimārgitavyaṁ) – "Then, that *Pada* should be sought out with diligence":

The term पदं (padaṁ) is rich in meaning—it can denote state, abode, goal, or station. Here, it refers to the Supreme Abode, the final destination of the soul, beyond saṁsāra, untouched by decay.

The prefix परिमार्गितव्यम् (to be thoroughly sought after) expresses intense and contemplative seeking, not superficial wandering but a साधना sādhana suffused with yearning and discernment.

— ॐ —

यस्मिन्गताः न निवर्तन्ति भूयः (yasmin gatāḥ na nivartanti bhūyaḥ) – "Having reached which, one does not return again":

This line evokes the doctrine of moksha. It declares the finality and absoluteness of liberation. Once the Jīva attains this पद Pada, there is no punarāvṛtti—no more return to the cycle of birth and death. This is the realm of the Real (sat), where the delusion of duality ends.

— ॐ —

तम् एव च आद्यं पुरुषं प्रपद्ये (tam eva cādyaṁ purushaṁ prapadye) – "I seek refuge in that Primal-Being alone":

The term आद्यं पुरुषं (ādyaṁ purushaṁ) refers to the Primordial-Being—the पुरुषोत्तम Puruṣottama, the Supreme Self beyond the क्षर kshara (perishable) and अक्षर akshara (imperishable).

To प्रपद्ये prapadye—to surrender—is not mere prostration but a sacred self-offering, the culmination of bhakti and jnāna, the dissolving of individuality into the Universal.

O mortal, let this little wave forever disappear—and may we verily become one within the waveless ocean of consciousness.

— ॐ —

यतः प्रवृत्तिः प्रसृता पुराणी (yataḥ pravṛttiḥ prasṛtā purāṇī) – "From whom the ancient movement has proceeded":

Here, प्रवृत्तिः pravṛttiḥ signifies the manifestation, the outward motion of creation, sustained by Māyā. It is termed पुराणी purāṇī—eternal and beginningless—reflecting the ageless process of cosmic emergence from the आद्य पुरुष Ādya-Purusha. This Source of ours is both transcendent and immanent.

We came from Him, and we will disappear back in Him one day—but why broker any delay?

—: In Brief :—

— ॐ श्रीकृष्णाय नमः ॐ —

The Blessed Lord has thus laid forth a sublime path: first, to transcend the web of entanglement by wielding the sword of वैराग्य vairāgya, thereby severing the binding threads of attachment and karma.

This decisive act of renunciation is but the prelude to the higher goal, the real pursuit—the wholehearted turning toward the आदि पुरुष Ādi-Purusha, the Supreme Spirit, the eternal ground from whom is our beingness and from where all creation has emerged.

— ॐ श्रीरामाय नमः ॐ —

This verse beautifully directs us to take refuge in the primordial essence Braham—whose manifest form is Bhagwāna Shri Krishna; to seek with unwavering commitment the supreme state that is beyond returns: the state of final emancipation where the soul, freed from all vestiges of duality and delusion, abides in his true, imperishable nature.

This is not merely an end but the fulfilment of the soul's deepest yearning: the realization of the immutable truth which lies beyond these fleeting plays of Māyā, outside the ambit of this manifest world.

In the next verse, the Lord graciously reveals the distinguishing marks of those exalted devotees who, having taken refuge in the Supreme Being, attain the highest goal of union with the Divine.

— ॐ तत सत ॐ —

Before we move on, let us bow in reverence to this sacred verse. Write it by hand, reflect on its meaning, chant it aloud, make it your own.

— ॐ —

ततः पदं तत्परिमार्गितव्यं यस्मिन्गता न निवर्तन्ति भूयः ।
tataḥ padaṁ tatparimārgitavyaṁ yasmingatā na nivartanti bhūyaḥ
तमेव चाद्यं पुरुषं प्रपद्ये यतः प्रवृत्तिः प्रसृता पुराणी ॥१५-४॥
tameva cādyaṁ puruṣaṁ prapadye yataḥ pravṛttiḥ prasṛtā purāṇī (15-4)

— ॐ —

ततः पदं तत्परिमार्गितव्यं यस्मिन्गता न निवर्तन्ति भूयः ।
tataḥ padaṁ tatparimārgitavyaṁ yasmingatā na nivartanti bhūyaḥ
तमेव चाद्यं पुरुषं प्रपद्ये यतः प्रवृत्तिः प्रसृता पुराणी ॥१५-४॥
tameva cādyaṁ puruṣaṁ prapadye yataḥ pravṛttiḥ prasṛtā purāṇī (15-4)

ॐ तत्सदिति श्रीमद्भगवद्गीतासूपनिषत्सु ब्रह्मविद्यायां योगशास्त्रे श्रीकृष्णार्जुनसंवादे
om tatsaditi śrīmadbhagavadgītāsūpaniṣatsu brahmavidyāyāṁ yogaśāstre śrīkṛṣṇārjunasaṁvāde
पुरुषोत्तमयोगो नाम पञ्चदशोऽध्यायः श्लोकः ४
puruṣottamayogo nāma pañcadaśo'dhyāyaḥ ślokaḥ 4

Om-Tat-Sat—Om (Braham) is the sole Reality. In the Yogic Scripture on the Science-of-Braham, the Shrimada-Bhāgvada-Gītā Upanishad, we hereby conclude Shloka 4 of the Dialogue between Shrī Krishna and Arjuna entitled Purushottama-Yoga, Canto XV.

— ॐ कौसल्यानन्दनाय नमः ॐ —

Not a Cry, But a Clarity
No pleading. No praise.
Only: "I Am Done Revolving. Enough Already."

— o —

He lays down names.
Takes up silence.
And silence answers.
ātmā never did hide.
Ye had only forgotten.

ॐ गीता श्लोकः १५.५ – GĪTĀ VERSE 15.5

ॐ श्रीमद्भगवद्गीतासूपनिषत्सु ब्रह्मविद्यायां योगशास्त्रे श्रीकृष्णार्जुनसंवादे
om śrīmadbhagavadgītāsūpaniṣatsu brahmavidyāyāṁ yogaśāstre śrīkṛṣṇārjunasaṁvāde
पुरुषोत्तमयोगो नाम पञ्चदशोऽध्यायः श्लोकः ५
puruṣottamayogo nāma pañcadaśo'dhyāyaḥ ślokaḥ 5

— ॐ —

निर्मानमोहा जितसङ्गदोषा अध्यात्मनित्या विनिवृत्तकामाः ।
nirmānamohā jitasaṅgadoṣā adhyātmanityā vinivṛttakāmāḥ
द्वन्द्वैर्विमुक्ताः सुखदुःखसंज्ञैर्गच्छन्त्यमूढाः पदमव्ययं तत् ॥ १५-५ ॥
dvandvairvimuktāḥ sukhaduḥkhasaṁjñair-
gacchantyamūḍhāḥ padamavyayaṁ tat (15-5)

Freed from pride and delusions, overcoming the evil of attachments, ever devoted to spiritual pursuits, altogether ceased of desires and rid of the throngs of dualities such as pleasures and pains—the wise will reach That Immortal State. (15.5)

—: Word-by-Word :—

निर्मानमोहाः nirmāna-mohāḥ – free from pride and delusion; जितसङ्गदोषाः jita-saṅga-doṣāḥ – having conquered the flaw of attachment; अध्यात्मनित्याः adhyātma-nityāḥ – ever devoted to spirituality; विनिवृत्तकामाः vinivṛtta-kāmāḥ – free from desires; द्वन्द्वैः dvandvaiḥ – from dualities; विमुक्ताः vimuktāḥ – liberated; सुखदुःखसंज्ञैः sukha-duḥkha-saṁjñaiḥ – known as pleasure and pain; गच्छन्ति gacchanti – they attain; अमूढाः amūḍhāḥ – the wise; पदम् padam – the state; अव्ययम् avyayam – imperishable; तत् tat – that.

—: Understanding The Verse :—

— ॐ श्रीकृष्णाय नमः ॐ —

This here verse is a luminous beacon within the sacred dialogue—for it reveals the inner disposition and spiritual stature of those rare souls who do manage to severe away the binding cords of worldly entanglements.

Here, Bhagwāna Shri Krishna delineates not just the outward signs of a seeker's progress but unveils the very essence of liberation—जीवन मुक्ति jīvanmukti—the living freedom that blossoms from profound inner renunciation.

The path described is not a philosophical abstraction—rather it is the living testament of those who, having turned their gaze unwaveringly toward the Supreme, become fully free from entanglements, delusions, and the snares of fleeting pleasures and pains.

— ॐ सर्वतीर्थमयाय नमः ॐ —

Such aspirants, by cultivating unwavering devotion and extinguishing the restless fires of desire, ascend to that imperishable state—the immortal abode, पदम् अव्ययम् padam avyayam—where dualities dissolve and only the oneness of the Divine-Realm remains.

This teaching affirms that liberation is not bestowed by mere ritual or intellectual assent but through a radical inner transformation—where the soul stands purified, luminous, and wholly devoted to the Supreme.

—: Key Sanskrit Terms :—

Let us explore the verse by focusing on the deeper implications of its key Sanskrit expressions:

— ॐ —

निर्मानमोहाः (nirmāna-mohāḥ) – “Freed from pride and delusion”:

- निर्मान Māna is pride, the self-assumption of superiority born of ego.

- मोह Moha is delusion, the misapprehension of the Real as the unreal. The prefix निर् *nir* (negation)- signifies complete freedom. The जीव Jīva who is निर्मानमोहाः nirmāna-moha has transcended ego, the false self, and the fog of illusion it carries . This is the first gate to freedom: the false identity of the self must be dropped for Truth to be known.

— ॐ —

जितसङ्गदोषाः (jita-saṅga-doṣāḥ) – “Having conquered the fault of attachment”:

- सङ्ग Saṅga is attachments, especially to vishayas (sense-objects), people, fruits (outcomes).

- दोष Doṣa implies impurity or fault. One who has जित jita (conquered) this is inwardly free. Attachment is not affection, but clinging born of identification. Its conquest purifies the अन्तःकरण antaḥkaraṇa—the inner instrument by which we know of the world around us.

— ॐ —

अध्यात्मनित्याः (adhyātma-nityāḥ) – “Ever devoted to the Self”:

- अध्यात्म Adhyātma refers to the Self or the spiritual principle.
- नित्य Nitya means constant, unceasing. This points to नित्य अभ्यास nitya-abhyāsa, unbroken contemplation of the true Self आत्म विचार (ātma-vichāra), the heart of ज्ञान योग jnāna-yoga: understanding who am I.

— ॐ —

विनिवृत्तकामाः (vinivṛtta-kāmāḥ) – "Desires completely withdrawn":

- काम Kāma is desire—stemming from wants and illusions, rooted in the false sense of the I, and ever leading to more incompleteness.
- विनिवृत्त Vinivṛtta signifies full withdrawal, cessation not through suppression but through wisdom. This is the natural fruit of inner fullness; desire dissolves when the Self is realized as complete.

— ॐ —

द्वन्द्वैः विमुक्ताः सुखदुःखसंज्ञैः (dvandvair vimuktāḥ sukha-duḥkha-saṁjñaiḥ) – "Freed from the dualities called pleasure and pain":

- द्वन्द्व Dvandva refers to all dualities—heat and cold, gain and loss, fame and blame.
- संज्ञैः Saṁjñāḥ means mental impressions or designations. To be free from द्वन्द्व dvandvas is to see things as mere fluctuations on the surface of Prakriti, without real impact on me—who am the साक्षी Sākṣin (the witnessing Self).

— ॐ —

अमूढाः (amūḍhāḥ) – "Undeluded":

मूढ Mūḍha means one bewildered, confused by माया Māyā.

अमूढ Amūḍha is the knower, the one whose discrimination has arisen. He walks no longer in darkness.

— ॐ —

गच्छन्ति पदम् अव्ययम् तत् (gacchanti padam avyayam tat) – "They reach That Immutable Abode":

- गच्छन्ति Gacchanti—they go, they attain.
- अव्ययम् Avyayam—imperishable, beyond decay.
- पदम् Padam—abode, state, station.

This पदम् padam is none other than Braham, the eternal, the blissful, the Reality beyond all becoming.

—: In Brief :—

We learn here that the journey of the liberated is marked by the cutting away of worldly illusions with the sharp sword of discriminative wisdom (viveka) and detachment (vairāgya).

The entanglement with body-consciousness—the deep-seated sense of "I" and "mine"—is the root of our endless desires, each one giving birth to yet another, in a ceaseless chain of longings, achievements, failures, ever higher goals and an unending dissatisfaction.

Having seen the ephemeral nature of all phenomenal existence, this fleeting play of name and form ceases for the wise—who no more seeks fulfilment in the impermanent.

With desires stilled and dualities transcended, the sage rests in the natural bliss of the Self, knowing his body, senses, mind, and intellect as mere instruments, and recognizing their transience.

— ॐ श्रीरामाय नमः ॐ —

Such an aspirant, absorbed in the Self, is utterly unmoved by the vicissitudes of pleasure and pain, gain and loss.

Having reached the brink of Supreme Reality, he stands at the threshold of that Eternal Abode, which the Lord goes on to describe in the following verse.

— ॐ तत सत ॐ —

Before we move on, let us bow in reverence to this sacred verse. Write it by hand, reflect on its meaning, chant it aloud, make it your own.

— ॐ —

निर्मानमोहा जितसङ्गदोषा अध्यात्मनित्या विनिवृत्तकामाः ।
nirmānamohā jitasaṅgadoṣā adhyātmanityā vinivṛttakāmāḥ
द्वन्द्वैर्विमुक्ताः सुखदुःखसंज्ञैर्गच्छन्त्यमूढाः पदमव्ययं तत् ॥ १५-५॥
dvandvairvimuktāḥ sukhaduḥkhasaṁjñairgacchantyamūḍhāḥ padamavyayaṁ tat (15-5)

— ॐ —

निर्मानमोहा जितसङ्गदोषा अध्यात्मनित्या विनिवृत्तकामाः ।
nirmānamohā jitasaṅgadoṣā adhyātmanityā vinivṛttakāmāḥ
द्वन्द्वैर्विमुक्ताः सुखदुःखसंज्ञैर्गच्छन्त्यमूढाः पदमव्ययं तत् ॥ १५-५ ॥
dvandvairvimuktāḥ sukhaduḥkhasaṁjñairgacchantyamūḍhāḥ padamavyayaṁ tat (15-5)

ॐ तत्सदिति श्रीमद्भगवद्गीतासूपनिषत्सु ब्रह्मविद्यायां योगशास्त्रे श्रीकृष्णार्जुनसंवादे
om tatsaditi śrīmadbhagavadgītāsūpaniṣatsu brahmavidyāyāṁ yogaśāstre śrīkṛṣṇārjunasaṁvāde
पुरुषोत्तमयोगो नाम पञ्चदशोऽध्यायः श्लोकः ५
puruṣottamayogo nāma pañcadaśo'dhyāyaḥ ślokaḥ 5

Om-Tat-Sat—Om (Braham) is the sole Reality. In the Yogic Scripture on the Science-of-Braham, the Shrimada-Bhāgvada-Gītā Upanishad, we hereby conclude Shloka 5 of the Dialogue between Shrī Krishna and Arjuna entitled Purushottama-Yoga, Canto XV.

ॐ गीता श्लोकः १५.६ – GĪTĀ VERSE 15.6

ॐ श्रीमद्भगवद्गीतासूपनिषत्सु ब्रह्मविद्यायां योगशास्त्रे श्रीकृष्णार्जुनसंवादे
om śrīmadbhagavadgītāsūpaniṣatsu brahmavidyāyāṁ yogaśāstre śrīkṛṣṇārjunasaṁvāde
पुरुषोत्तमयोगो नाम पञ्चदशोऽध्यायः श्लोकः ६
puruṣottamayogo nāma pañcadaśo'dhyāyaḥ ślokaḥ 6

— ॐ —

न तद्भासयते सूर्यो न शशाङ्को न पावकः ।
na tadbhāsayate sūryo na śaśāṅko na pāvakaḥ
यद्गत्वा न निवर्तन्ते तद्धाम परमं मम ॥ १५-६ ॥
yadgatvā na nivartante taddhāma paramaṁ mama (15-6)

The sun does not illumine That; nor the moon or fire. That supreme self-effulgent sphere—attaining Which there is no more return to the world—That is my Supreme-Abode. (15.6)

—: Word-by-Word :—

न na – not; तत् tat – that; भासयते bhāsayate – illuminates; सूर्यः sūryaḥ – the sun; न na – nor; शशाङ्कः śaśāṅkaḥ – the moon; न na – nor; पावकः pāvakaḥ – fire; यत् yat – which; गत्वा gatvā – having reached; न निवर्तन्ते na nivartante – they do not return; तत् tat – that; धाम dhāma – abode; परमम् paramam – supreme; मम mama – My.

—: Understanding The Verse :—

— ॐ श्रीकृष्णाय नमः ॐ —

This beautiful verse 15.6 breathes the ineffable majesty of the Supreme Reality, the परम धाम Paraṁ Dhāma, the transcendent abode which lies beyond the reach of mortal perception.

Here, Shri Krishna lifts the veil, granting Arjuna—and through him, all us seekers—a fleeting glimpse into the realm which is self-effulgent, untouched by the borrowed brilliance of sun, moon, or fire.

This is no mystical vision—rather it is the ultimate goal of all spiritual striving, the radiant core of सनातन धर्म Sanātana-Dharma, where the jīva, having cast aside the chains of संसार saṁsāra, finds his true eternal home.

— ॐ पराकाशाय नमः ॐ —

The preceding verse spoke of the inner purification and detachment required to ascend toward liberation, and now Bhagwāna Shri Krishna reveals the sublime destination of such a purified soul: His own imperishable abode, the eternal realm of sat-cit-ānanda, where all dualities dissolve, and the seeker finds himself in perfect union with the Supreme-Being.

It is this supreme reality—Krishna's own transcendental abode—that, once attained, admits no return to the bondage of worldly existence.

—: Key Sanskrit Terms :—

In the hush of reflection, let us dwell upon the verse's Sanskrit jewels, each radiating quiet ripples of deeper meanings.

— ॐ —

न तद्भासयते सूर्यः (na tat bhāsayate sūryaḥ) – "The sun does not illumine That":

सूर्यः Sūryaḥ, symbol of the physical and subtle light, is the lord of the manifest day.
Yet, it cannot भासयते bhāsayate—it cannot reveal or illuminate That Supreme Reality. For That-One is *self-luminous* स्वयं प्रकाश *(svayamprakāśa)*, needing no external light to be perceived.

— ॐ —

न शशाङ्कः (na śaśāṅkaḥ) – "Nor the moon":

शशाङ्कः Śaśāṅkaḥ—the moon, lord of coolness, serenity, and reflective illumination.
The moon, symbol of soothing, gentle light, cannot illumine That-One which transcends both brilliance and gentleness.

— ॐ —

न पावकः (na pāvakaḥ) – "Nor fire":

पावकः Pāvakaḥ, fire, the element of transformation and illumination, also fails to cast its light upon the Supreme.
Fire, the primal energy, is but a flickering shadow before the eternal radiance of *Braham* whose manifest form is Krishna.

— ॐ —

यद्गत्वा न निवर्तन्ते (yad gatvā na nivartante) – "Going where, they do not return":

The way to That Supreme is absolute and final—one way and with no return.

From There, there is no *punarāvṛtti* (return to this saṁsāra).

The *Jīva* attains absolute liberation *(moksha)*—complete freedom from the cycle of births-deaths in which he had stayed revolving for eons.

— ॐ —

तत् धाम परमं मम (tat dhāma paramaṁ mama) – "That is My Supreme Abode":

धाम Dhāma means abode, but here it also conveys *effulgence, essence,* and *dwelling-place* of the spirit.

परमं Paramam—supreme, beyond comparison.

मम Mama—Krishna declares it as His own ultimate nature, the final Reality called सच्चिदानन्द ब्रह्म satt-chitt-ānanda braham, beyond His manifest form as Krishna.

Thus, the verse sets aside all earthly and celestial lights, pointing directly to the eternal self-luminous Braham, which is Krishna's own परम स्वरूप *Paraṁ-Svarūpa*.

—: *In Brief* :—

— ॐ श्रीकृष्णाय नमः ॐ —

In this exalted utterance, the Lord solemnly declares: "That is My Supreme Abode, reaching which none return to the transient world."

Here, the Supreme-One speaks not of a distant celestial realm but of the very essence of divine existence—His own eternal nature—radiant and self-luminous, beyond this material show of lights and shadows.

— ॐ श्रीरामाय नमः ॐ —

The path laid out in the previous verses now finds its culmination in this vision of the Supreme Goal.

Yet, as the Lord prepares to deepen the discourse, a profound question arises: If the soul, too, is of the same divine essence, why does it not spontaneously abide in that supreme state?

This question forms the natural bridge to the next verse, where the Lord elucidates the nature of the jīva—describing it as none other than the eternal itself, a fragment of His own Self—a ripple amongst countless ripples in the lake below -- which's reflecting just the one Moon above.

— ॐ परस्मै ज्योतिषे नमः ॐ —

Verse 15.6 serves as the vital link between the path of purification (described in verse 15.5) and the revelation of the soul's intrinsic nature (in verse 15.7), weaving the tapestry of the chapter into a seamless progression toward the highest wisdom.

Though this teaching finds fuller exposition in verse 15.12, the present verse is masterfully placed to bind the preceding and forthcoming teachings into one cohesive vision of the jīva's journey to his eternal Source.

— ॐ तत सत ॐ —

Before we move on, let us bow in reverence to this sacred verse—a timeless beacon of wisdom guiding seekers for ages. Write it by hand, reflect on its meaning, and chant it aloud, for these sounds alone carry the authenticity of that era. The world may have changed but the living vibration of these Sanskrit sounds still remain as original as they were when Bhagwān Shri Krishna Himself walked the earth and imparted these teachings.

— ॐ —

न तद्भासयते सूर्यो न शशाङ्को न पावकः ।
na tadbhāsayate sūryo na śaśāṅko na pāvakaḥ
यद्गत्वा न निवर्तन्ते तद्धाम परमं मम ॥ १५-६ ॥
yadgatvā na nivartante taddhāma paramaṁ mama (15-6)

— ॐ —

न तद्भासयते सूर्यो न शशाङ्को न पावकः ।
na tadbhāsayate sūryo na śaśāṅko na pāvakaḥ
यद्गत्वा न निवर्तन्ते तद्धाम परमं मम ॥ १५-६ ॥
yadgatvā na nivartante taddhāma paramaṁ mama (15-6)

ॐ तत्सदिति श्रीमद्भगवद्गीतासूपनिषत्सु ब्रह्मविद्यायां योगशास्त्रे श्रीकृष्णार्जुनसंवादे
om tatsaditi śrīmadbhagavadgītāsūpaniṣatsu brahmavidyāyāṁ yogaśāstre śrīkṛṣṇārjunasaṁvāde
पुरुषोत्तमयोगो नाम पञ्चदशोऽध्यायः श्लोकः ६
puruṣottamayogo nāma pañcadaśo'dhyāyaḥ ślokaḥ 6

Om-Tat-Sat—Om (Braham) is the sole Reality. In the Yogic Scripture on the Science-of-Braham, the Shrimada-Bhāgvada-Gītā Upanishad, we hereby conclude Shloka 6 of the Dialogue between Shrī Krishna and Arjuna entitled Purushottama-Yoga, Canto XV.

— ॐ दामोदराय नमः ॐ —

All Lights End

The lamp glows—then flickers and dies.
The sun sinks. Fire fades. The moon forgets.
But That One ever remains—
No smoke,
No ash,
Ever lit, One Undimmed Fiery Brilliance—spanning from Eternity to Eternity.

ॐ गीता श्लोकः १५.७ – GĪTĀ VERSE 15.7

ॐ श्रीमद्भगवद्गीतासूपनिषत्सु ब्रह्मविद्यायां योगशास्त्रे श्रीकृष्णार्जुनसंवादे
om śrīmadbhagavadgītāsūpaniṣatsu brahmavidyāyāṁ yogaśāstre śrīkṛṣṇārjunasaṁvāde
पुरुषोत्तमयोगो नाम पञ्चदशोऽध्यायः श्लोकः ७
puruṣottamayogo nāma pañcadaśo'dhyāyaḥ ślokaḥ 7

— ॐ —

ममैवांशो जीवलोके जीवभूतः सनातनः ।
mamaivāṁśo jīvaloke jīvabhūtaḥ sanātanaḥ
मनःषष्ठानीन्द्रियाणि प्रकृतिस्थानि कर्षति ॥ १५-७ ॥
manaḥṣaṣṭhānīndriyāṇi prakṛtisthāni karṣati (15-7)

Verily a fragment of my Self, having become this eternal embodied soul—the *Jīvātmā*—draws around itself the mind and the five senses which rest in Nature. (15.7)

—: *Word-by-Word* :—

मम mama – My; एव eva – indeed; अंशः aṁśaḥ – fragment; जीवलोके jīva-loke – in the world of living beings; जीवभूतः jīva-bhūtaḥ – becoming the individual soul; सनातनः sanātanaḥ – eternal; मनःषष्ठानि manaḥ-ṣaṣṭhāni – with the mind as the sixth; इन्द्रियाणि indriyāṇi – the senses; प्रकृतिस्थानि prakriti-sthāni – situated in nature; कर्षति karṣati – draws.

—: *Understanding The Verse* :—

— ॐ श्रीकृष्णाय नमः ॐ —

Verse 15.7 again shines as a revelation of deep metaphysical truth, wherein Shri Krishna discloses the intimate bond between the individual soul (Jīva) and the Supreme Self—that they are both the same.

In this verse, the veil is lifted upon the mystery of embodiment: how a spark of the Divine, though eternally pure and infinite in essence, becomes ensnared in the play of Prakriti—drawing around itself the mind and the senses, and thus taking on the appearance of individuality: the individual soul, or the Jīva.

— ॐ श्रीरामाय नमः ॐ —

The Lord, in His infinite compassion, reveals that the Jīva, though a mere fragment अंश (aṁśa) of His own Self, is nevertheless endowed with the faculties that tether it to worldly existence.

This verse resounds with the profound dialogue between the finite and the Infinite, between the imperishable essence of the soul and the transient vestures it dons in the field of Nature.

Like an actor who assumes various roles on the stage, the Jīva takes on the guise of embodied existence—seemingly bound and entangled in worldly names and forms, though his intrinsic nature remains untouched and ever one with the Supreme.

—: Key Sanskrit Terms :—

Let us explore the verse by focusing on the deeper implications of its key Sanskrit expressions:

— ॐ —

मम एव अंशः (mama eva aṁśaḥ) – "Verily, a portion of Mine":

- मम Mama = "of Me", एव eva = "surely", अंशः aṁśaḥ = "portion, spark, ray".

Krishna speaks not metaphorically but ontologically—the Jīva is not separate, but a part of the Divine. However, this is not a physical division; it is akin to a ray from the sun—not cut off, but appearing distinct due to उपाधि upādhis (limiting adjuncts).

— ॐ —

जीवलोके जीवभूतः (jīvaloke jīvabhūtaḥ) – "In the world of beings, becoming the living soul":

- जीवलोक Jīvaloka refers to the empirical realm where sentient beings dwell.

- जीवभूतः Jīvabhūtaḥ indicates the जीव Jīva—the individualized soul, endowed with अहंकार ahaṅkāra (ego) and agency, the idea of being a doer, an agent.

Upon entering the संसार saṁsāra, this Divine portion dons the identity of the जीव Jīva and gets sucked into the world, staying entangled in the phenomenal worlds of names and forms until the day he wakes up from his stupor.

— ॐ —

सनातनः (sanātanaḥ) – "Eternal":

The Jīva is beginningless and deathless, not a transient product of matter. Though he forgets his nature, he is never destroyed, never born. This word reflects the deepest truths of सनातन धर्म Sanātana-

Dharma—that the individual soul, though embodied, is of the same eternal essence as the Absolute.

— ॐ —

मनःषष्ठानि इन्द्रियाणि (manaḥ-ṣaṣṭhāni indriyāṇi) – "The mind and the five senses":

- षष्ठ Ṣaṣṭha means "sixth"—thus, the mind is counted as the sixth sense. The senses are not merely physical organs but subtle faculties, directed outward.

- मनः manaḥ—mind—functions as their coordinator, interpreting and responding.

These six are instruments through which the जीव Jīva experiences प्रकृति Prakriti or the world.

— ॐ —

प्रकृतिस्थानि कर्षति (prakritisthāni karṣati) – "Attracts and pulls them, situated in Nature":

- प्रकृतिस्थानि Prakriti-sthāni = those faculties grounded in Nature.

- कर्षति Karṣati = draws, pulls, or drags—an evocative verb signifying the effort and struggle of embodiment.

The जीव Jīva, having entered into प्रकृति Prakriti, is burdened with the task of animating these instruments, drawn by impressions and impulses from past karma.

—: In Brief :—

— ॐ श्रीकृष्णाय नमः ॐ —

In this sacred utterance, Shri Krishna lays bare the nature of the Jīva as a fragment—अंश aṁśa—of the Supreme Being, an eternal spark of the infinite Braham -- whose manifest form is Krishna Himself.

Though the Supreme dwells in His fullness as सत-चित-आनन्द sat-cit-ānanda—the eternal, conscious, blissful Reality—the जीव Jīva, as a finite reflection, moves through the cycles of birth and rebirth, bound to the world by the faculties it has drawn unto itself: the mind and the five senses, which are themselves products of Prakriti.

These instruments, though appearing to empower the Jīva, are mere channels through which it engages the external world, while the true power behind all action and perception remains ever that of the Supreme.

— ॐ श्रीरामाय नमः ॐ —

This verse illumines the paradox of the Jīva's existence: though divine in essence, he is deluded into identification with these transient coverings. It is only through self-knowledge and divine grace that the Jīva can transcend this illusion and realize his oneness with the Supreme.

Thus, while the Jīva appears to act and experience independently, it is, in truth, ever dependent upon the Lord-God, who is the ultimate source of all life and movement.

— ॐ सत्यवाचे नमः ॐ —

Leading into the next verse, Bhagwāna Shri Krishna now turns to illustrate how, having identified with the mind and senses, the Jīva roams from one embodiment to another, wandering through countless births.

This journey of the soul, driven by its attachments and identifications, is vividly described by Shri Krishna through a striking simile which deepens our understanding of the soul's entanglement in संसार saṁsāra.

— ॐ तत सत ॐ —

Before we move on, let us bow in reverence to this sacred verse. Write it by hand, reflect on its meaning, chant it aloud, make it your own.

— ॐ —

ममैवांशो जीवलोके जीवभूतः सनातनः ।
mamaivāṁśo jīvaloke jīvabhūtaḥ sanātanaḥ
मनःषष्ठानीन्द्रियाणि प्रकृतिस्थानि कर्षति ॥१५-७॥
manaḥṣaṣṭhānīndriyāṇi prakṛtisthāni karṣati (15-7)

— ॐ —

ममैवांशो जीवलोके जीवभूतः सनातनः ।
mamaivāṁśo jīvaloke jīvabhūtaḥ sanātanaḥ
मनःषष्ठानीन्द्रियाणि प्रकृतिस्थानि कर्षति ॥१५-७॥
manaḥṣaṣṭhānīndriyāṇi prakṛtisthāni karṣati (15-7)

ॐ तत्सदिति श्रीमद्भगवद्गीतासूपनिषत्सु ब्रह्मविद्यायां योगशास्त्रे श्रीकृष्णार्जुनसंवादे
om tatsaditi śrīmadbhagavadgītāsūpaniṣatsu brahmavidyāyāṁ yogaśāstre śrīkṛṣṇārjunasaṁvāde
पुरुषोत्तमयोगो नाम पञ्चदशोऽध्यायः श्लोकः ७
puruṣottamayogo nāma pañcadaśo'dhyāyaḥ ślokaḥ 7

Om-Tat-Sat—Om (Braham) is the sole Reality. In the Yogic Scripture on the Science-of-Braham, the Shrimada-Bhāgvada-Gītā Upanishad, we hereby conclude Shloka 7 of the Dialogue between Shrī Krishna and Arjuna entitled Purushottama-Yoga, Canto XV.

ॐ गीता श्लोकः १५.८ – GĪTĀ VERSE 15.8

ॐ श्रीमद्भगवद्गीतासूपनिषत्सु ब्रह्मविद्यायां योगशास्त्रे श्रीकृष्णार्जुनसंवादे
om śrīmadbhagavadgītāsūpaniṣatsu brahmavidyāyāṁ yogaśāstre śrīkṛṣṇārjunasaṁvāde
पुरुषोत्तमयोगो नाम पञ्चदशोऽध्यायः श्लोकः ८
puruṣottamayogo nāma pañcadaśo'dhyāyaḥ ślokaḥ 8

— ॐ —

शरीरं यदवाप्नोति यच्चाप्युत्क्रामतीश्वरः ।
śarīraṁ yadavāpnoti yaccāpyutkrāmatīśvaraḥ
गृहीत्वैतानि संयाति वायुर्गन्धानिवाशयात् ॥१५-८॥
gṛhītvaitāni saṁyāti vāyurgandhānivāśayāt (15-8)

Upon dropping the body behind, when the *Jīvātmā* migrates to a new body, it goes carrying away these (the mind and the senses spoken above)—just as the breeze wafts the odors away from their seats, bearing them along with it.
(15.8)

—: *Word-by-Word* :—

शरीरम् śarīram – the body; यत् yat – which; अवाप्नोति avāpnoti – acquires; यत् yat – which; च api – and also; उत्क्रामति utkrāmati – leaves; ईश्वरः īśvaraḥ – the lord (soul); गृहीत्वा gṛhītvā – taking; एतानि etāni – these (senses); संयाति saṁyāti – goes; वायुः vāyuḥ – like the wind; गन्धान् gandhān – scents; इव iva – as; आशयात् āśayāt – from their source (like flowers).

—: *Understanding The Verse* :—

— ॐ श्रीकृष्णाय नमः ॐ —

In this verse Shri Krishna further deepens Arjuna's understanding of the soul's journey through the cycles of birth and death.

Here, the Lord employs a vivid and poetic analogy—the breeze wafting fragrances from their source—to illustrate how the Jīva, upon casting off one body, carries with it the subtle faculties of mind and senses onto new embodiments while he journeys on.

— ॐ श्रीरामाय नमः ॐ —

Though it may appear that the Jīva acts by his own strength and volition, the Lord reveals that it is He Himself—Braham, whose manifest form is Krishna—who empowers and impels the Jīva at every stage, at each and every moment of his existence.

Just as the wind is untouched by the scents it carries, the soul, in its true nature, remains untouched by the bodily vestures it assumes.

Yet, by mistaking the instruments of Prakriti—the senses, mind, and body—to be his own, the Jīva becomes entangled in this endless mess, this wheel of saṁsāra.

— ॐ कंसारयाय नमः ॐ —

Through this teaching, Shri Krishna gently but firmly reminds us seekers that while the soul is a fragment of the Divine, yet he remains utterly dependent upon the Supreme for his movements, his very existence—and also that he does retain the sacred power of discernment to free himself from the snares of संसार saṁsāra.

—: Key Sanskrit Terms :—

Let us dwell upon the key Sanskrit terms to unravel the delicate strands of meaning woven into this śloka:

— ॐ —

शरीरम् (śarīram) – This term denotes the body, but in Vedāntic parlance, it is the देह deha, that which is subject to दहन dahana (burning, dissolution), implying its perishable and temporary nature. The शरीर śarīra is merely the upādhi (limiting adjunct) for the जीव jīva's functioning in the empirical world.

— ॐ —

यदवाप्नोति (yad avāpnoti) – Literally, "that which it attains."

This verb highlights the notion of assumption or acquisition, suggesting that the soul enters into or takes on the body—not by coercion, but through the momentum of past karma and latent impressions वासना (vāsanās).

— ॐ —

उत्क्रामति (utkrāmati) – Signifying the act of departure or ascension, this word is often used in the context of the soul leaving the gross body at the time of death.

It connotes the subtle process by which the embodied self जीवात्मा (jīvātman) exits its current corporeal frame.

— ॐ —

ईश्वरः (īśvaraḥ) – Here, the term is used to denote the individual soul or जीव jīva—in the sense of the doer, the controller of the body-mind-sense complex—he who is the 'enjoyer', the experiencer.

This is a subtle usage—while in many contexts ईश्वर Īśvara refers to the Supreme Lord, here it is employed in a relative sense, indicating the sovereign of the body, though still under the sway of माया māyā.

— ॐ —

गृहित्वैतानि (gṛhītvaitāni) – "Having taken these" – refers to the सूक्ष्म शरीर sūkṣma-śarīra (subtle body), primarily the mind मानस (manas), intellect बुद्धि (buddhi), and senses इन्द्रियाणि (indriyāṇi).

These travel along with the जीव jīva from one body to another, carried like a fragrance by the wind.

— ॐ —

वायुः (vāyuḥ) – The wind, symbolizing the unseen yet powerful force that conveys scent. This is a metaphor for the jīva's subtle movement, governed by the unseen law of karma.

वायु Vāyu is also associated with प्राण prāṇa, the vital force, linking the physiological to the metaphysical.

— ॐ —

गन्धान् (gandhān) – Scents or odors; metaphorically, the impressions or tendencies (saṁskāras) carried from one life to the next.

Just as fragrance clings to the breeze, so too the mental impressions of all his lifetimes cling to the soul.

— ॐ —

आशयात् (āśayāt) – From the receptacle, or source.

This refers to the previous body, the seat where the senses and mind were operative. Upon departure, the जीव jīva leaves that seat behind, taking the subtle essence of his experiences and impressions forward on his journey.

—: In Brief :—

— ॐ श्रीकृष्णाय नमः ॐ —

This verse powerfully affirms the delicate balance between divine ordainment and human responsibility. While the embodied soul is ever propelled by the will of the Supreme, he is also endowed with the sacred gift of discrimination by which he can free himself.

Each Jīva, by his own freedom, may either remain bound to the insentient coverings of body, mind, and senses, or through right understanding, renounce its false identification with these transient vehicles he happens to be riding on in this life.

Liberation is not achieved by external means alone but by a profound inner awakening—a resolute shift from misidentification with Prakriti's evolutes to steadfast realization of one's true nature—as being identical with the Divine.

— ॐ श्रीरामाय नमः ॐ —

Shri Krishna reveals that the human being's privilege lies in this power of discernment: to utilize the body and senses as instruments on the path of liberation, rather than falling into the illusion of mastery and, thereby, slavery to them.

Thus, what was granted for sacred purpose becomes, by error of attachment, a cause of bondage—until corrected by wisdom, discrimination, dispassion, surrender.

— ॐ दयासिन्धवे नमः ॐ —

In seamless progression, the Lord now moves to elucidate the expression मनः शष्ठाणि इन्द्रियाणी "manaḥ-ṣaṣṭhānīndriyāṇi"—the sixfold ensemble of mind and senses—shedding deeper light on their function and nature, and which is the subject of the next verse.

— ॐ तत सत ॐ —

Before we move on, let us bow in reverence to this sacred verse. Write it by hand, reflect on its meaning, chant it aloud, make it your own.

— ॐ —

शरीरं यदवाप्नोति यच्चाप्युत्क्रामतीश्वरः ।
śarīraṁ yadavāpnoti yaccāpyutkrāmatīśvaraḥ
गृहीत्वैतानि संयाति वायुर्गन्धानिवाशयात् ॥ १५-८ ॥
gṛhītvaitāni saṁyāti vāyurgandhānivāśayāt (15-8)

— ॐ —

शरीरं यदवाप्नोति यच्चाप्युत्क्रामतीश्वरः ।
śarīraṁ yadavāpnoti yaccāpyutkrāmatīśvaraḥ
गृहीत्वैतानि संयाति वायुर्गन्धानिवाशयात् ॥ १५-८ ॥
gṛhītvaitāni saṁyāti vāyurgandhānivāśayāt (15-8)

ॐ तत्सदिति श्रीमद्भगवद्गीतासूपनिषत्सु ब्रह्मविद्यायां योगशास्त्रे श्रीकृष्णार्जुनसंवादे
om tatsaditi śrīmadbhagavadgītāsūpaniṣatsu brahmavidyāyāṁ yogaśāstre śrīkṛṣṇārjunasaṁvāde
पुरुषोत्तमयोगो नाम पञ्चदशोऽध्यायः श्लोकः ८
puruṣottamayogo nāma pañcadaśo'dhyāyaḥ ślokaḥ 8

Om-Tat-Sat—Om (Braham) is the sole Reality. In the Yogic Scripture on the Science-of-Braham, the Shrimada-Bhāgvada-Gītā Upanishad, we hereby conclude Shloka 8 of the Dialogue between Shrī Krishna and Arjuna entitled Purushottama-Yoga, Canto XV.

ॐ गीता श्लोकः १५.९ – GĪTĀ VERSE 15.9

ॐ श्रीमद्भगवद्गीतासूपनिषत्सु ब्रह्मविद्यायां योगशास्त्रे श्रीकृष्णार्जुनसंवादे
om śrīmadbhagavadgītāsūpaniṣatsu brahmavidyāyāṁ yogaśāstre śrīkṛṣṇārjunasaṁvāde
पुरुषोत्तमयोगो नाम पञ्चदशोऽध्यायः श्लोकः ९
puruṣottamayogo nāma pañcadaśo'dhyāyaḥ ślokaḥ 9

— ॐ —

श्रोत्रं चक्षुः स्पर्शनं च रसनं घ्राणमेव च ।
śrotraṁ cakṣuḥ sparśanaṁ ca rasanaṁ ghrāṇameva ca
अधिष्ठाय मनश्चायं विषयानुपसेवते ॥ १५-९ ॥
adhiṣṭhāya manaścāyaṁ viṣayānupasevate (15-9)

Presiding over the sense-organs of hearing, sight, touch, taste and smell, as also the mind, it is the *Jīvātmā* who is the partaker of sense-enjoyments through the instrument of the body wherein he currently dwells. (15.9)

—: *Word-by-Word* :—

श्रोत्रम् śrotram – ear; चक्षुः cakṣuḥ – eye; स्पर्शनम् sparśanam – touch; च ca – and; रसनम् rasanam – taste; घ्राणम् ghrāṇam – smell; एव ca – indeed; अधिष्ठाय adhiṣṭhāya – presiding over; मनः manas – mind; च ca – and; अयम् ayam – this (soul); विषयान् viṣayān – sense objects; उपसेवते upasevate – enjoys.

—: *Understanding The Verse* :—

— ॐ श्रीकृष्णाय नमः ॐ —

Here's yet another verse standing as the luminous beacon within the sacred discourse of the Bhagavad-Gītā, which illumines the profound mystery of the embodied self—the जीवात्मा Jīvātmā—and his engagements with the world of sensory experiences.

Shri Krishna unveils the subtle mechanics of perception, whereby the जीवात्मा Jīvātmā, though inherently pure and untouched, presides over the ensemble of sense-organs—hearing, sight, touch, taste, and smell—along with the ever-restless mind.

Through his association with these instruments, the untouched unswayed soul—who alas has now become encased within this bodily frame—becomes not only the partaker of the manifold objects of the senses but views himself as the performer of karmas—as being an agent, the doer who is carrying the world upon his shoulders, and if he were to stop, then the whole world would come crashing down around him—although in truth he cannot control the functioning of even a single cells within his body, and everything carries on, as Krishna says, by dint of the Gunas enacting the whole show of nature —that happens to be running on an auto-pilot.

Fact remains: the जीव jīva is merely the experiencer—the being out on this joyride partaking of experiences good and bad; and hopefully one day he will get tired of this crazy show and just get up and head for Home—which is the Infinite Bliss of Krishna.

— ॐ कुरुक्षेत्रनायकाय नमः ॐ —

In this verse the Lord hints at a very deep truth: it is not the mere physical act of sensing that defines experience, but rather the intimate conjunction of the Self with the mind that animates and colors perceptions.

Without the mind's participation, the senses remain inert; and without the Ātmā's presence, both mind and senses are but lifeless. Thus, this verse gently exposes the entanglement of the soul in the saṃsāra, revolving in this cycle of birth and death—not by his own nature, but by his identification with the transient play of mind and senses.

When the last word has been spoken, all bondages upon the soul are found to be self-imposed.

— ॐ श्रीकृष्णाय परमात्मने नमः ॐ —

Shri Krishna subtly guides us seekers to reflect upon this Truth: that although it appears that the Jīvātmā enjoys or suffers through the senses, his true essence remains ever-untouched, pure, and luminous.

The embodied soul's seeming bondage is born not from his intrinsic nature, but from his mistaken association with the instruments of perception and the fleeting pleasures and pains they deliver.

—: *Key Sanskrit Terms* :—

Let us examine the verse. Let us trust its layered terms. Some meanings rise easily; others remain quiet beneath the surface, like pearls in silt. The Sanskrit teaches patience, not arrival.

— ॐ —

श्रोत्र (śrotram) – The faculty of hearing, not merely the physical ear but the इन्द्रिय indriya (sense organ) that apprehends sound शब्द (śabda).

It is शब्द तन्मात्र प्रधान śabda-tanmātra-pradhāna, connected to the element of आकाश *ākāśa* (ether).

— ॐ —

चक्षुः (cakṣuḥ) – The faculty of sight, associated with रुप rūpa (form) and तेज *tejas* (fire).

It symbolizes perception of external phenomena and is central to attachment in the world of forms.

— ॐ —

स्पर्शनं (sparśanam) – The sense of touch, seated in the skin (tvak), linked with *vāyu* (air).

It reveals both contact and subtle forms of interaction between subject and object.

— ॐ —

रसनं (rasanam) – The faculty of taste, linked to *jala* (water).

Taste is a direct and intimate form of sense experience, evocative of desire and indulgence.

— ॐ —

घ्राणम् (ghrāṇam) – The faculty of smell, rooted in *pṛthvī* (earth).

It suggests both subtle perception and deep-rooted tendencies वासना (vāsanās), as scent lingers and leaves impressions.

— ॐ —

अधिष्ठाय (adhiṣṭhāya) – "Having presided over" or "abiding in control."

This implies not passive residence but active rulership. The jīva, seated in the heart, governs these faculties via the subtle body.

— ॐ —

मनः (manaḥ) – The mind, the inner coordinator अन्तःकरण (antahkaraṇa), which not only processes sensory input but also serves as the seat of desire and deliberation.

Without the mind, the senses are inert.

— ॐ —

अयं (ayam) – "This one" – a reference to the individual soul जीवात्मा (jīvātman), not as a new entity, but as the same wanderer mentioned in the previous verse, continuing its engagement through a new bodily instrument.

— ॐ —

विषयान् (viṣayān) – "Objects of sense."

विषय Vishaya denotes not merely external objects but the entire field of sensory engagement. It also connotes temptation and bondage—what the soul becomes entangled with.

— ॐ —

उपसेवते (upasevate) – "Enjoys" or "partakes in," but more precisely, "serves" or "engages with."

This word subtly evokes **सेवना** sevanā, the act of indulgence. It hints at the subservience of the jīva to sensory allurements under the spell of **अविद्या** avidyā.

—: In Brief :—

— ॐ श्रीकृष्णाय नमः ॐ —

In brief, this verse impresses upon the thoughtful aspirant the dual reality: the transient play of sense-experiences and the eternal stillness of the Self.

Though the senses tirelessly gather impressions and the mind weaves them into the fabric of experiences, the Jīvātmā—sentient, eternal, and pure—remains ever-aloof, merely illuminating the play without itself being tainted by it.

Just as the sun shines upon all, yet remains unsoiled by the impurities of the earth, so too the Self witnesses pleasures and pains, yet is neither gladdened nor afflicted by them in any lasting way.

— ॐ श्रीरामाय नमः ॐ —

O mortal, heat and cold come and go, they never affect thee at thy core. You experience them and you move on, untouched.

Reflecting deeper, one realizes that no matter how many delightful sights have danced before these eyes, or how many bitter and sweet tastes have crossed the tongue, the Self remains unchanged—its essence untouched by contact with the world.

This discernment reveals the root of bondage: the soul, through entanglement with the mind and senses, assumes the pleasures and pains as if his own, mistaking the flickering for the real.

— ॐ संकर्षणाय नमः ॐ —

Thus, Shri Krishna tenderly reminds us that the true aim of human embodiment is not the mere pursuit of sensory gratification, which binds one further to the wheel of birth and death, but the realization of the Self's transcendence and ultimate liberation.

In the next verse, the Lord transitions from describing the soul's interaction with the senses to who truly perceives this subtle truth of the Self, and who, ensnared in ignorance, fails to discern it.

— ॐ तत सत ॐ —

Before we move on, let us bow in reverence to this sacred verse. Write it by hand, reflect on its meaning, chant it aloud, make it your own.

— ॐ —

श्रोत्रं चक्षुः स्पर्शनं च रसनं घ्राणमेव च ।
śrotraṁ cakṣuḥ sparśanaṁ ca rasanaṁ ghrāṇameva ca
अधिष्ठाय मनश्चायं विषयानुपसेवते ॥ १५-९॥
adhiṣṭhāya manaścāyaṁ viṣayānupasevate (15-9)

— ॐ —

श्रोत्रं चक्षुः स्पर्शनं च रसनं घ्राणमेव च ।
śrotraṁ cakṣuḥ sparśanaṁ ca rasanaṁ ghrāṇameva ca
अधिष्ठाय मनश्चायं विषयानुपसेवते ॥ १५-९ ॥
adhiṣṭhāya manaścāyaṁ viṣayānupasevate (15-9)

ॐ तत्सदिति श्रीमद्भगवद्गीतासूपनिषत्सु ब्रह्मविद्यायां योगशास्त्रे श्रीकृष्णार्जुनसंवादे
om tatsaditi śrīmadbhagavadgītāsūpaniṣatsu brahmavidyāyāṁ yogaśāstre śrīkṛṣṇārjunasaṁvāde
पुरुषोत्तमयोगो नाम पञ्चदशोऽध्यायः श्लोकः ९
puruṣottamayogo nāma pañcadaśo'dhyāyaḥ ślokaḥ 9

Om-Tat-Sat—Om (Braham) is the sole Reality. In the Yogic Scripture on the Science-of-Braham, the Shrimada-Bhāgvada-Gītā Upanishad, we hereby conclude Shloka 9 of the Dialogue between Shrī Krishna and Arjuna entitled Purushottama-Yoga, Canto XV.

— ॐ कर्णामृताय नमः ॐ —

No pleasure-garden is this Tree-of-World, no joy of Eden fair—
It is a maze of mirrored forms and long forgot love-pain, worry-care.
Each branch reflects the soul's own urge, each leaf a Vritti made;
And every flower a woven thought—that Time eventually sees decayed.
To love the Tree is to love that thing—which dies a thousand ways,
To touch its bark is to yearn and feel—throbs of long-forgotten days.
Yet still we climb, and still we reach, and still we refuse to see—
That all we seek upon this Tree—is what soon shall cease to be.

— o —

Be freed, O mortal,
Only he who seeks the Self itself,
gets the taste of true-bliss one day.

ॐ गीता श्लोकः १५.१० – Gītā Verse 15.10

ॐ श्रीमद्भगवद्गीतासूपनिषत्सु ब्रह्मविद्यायां योगशास्त्रे श्रीकृष्णार्जुनसंवादे
om śrīmadbhagavadgītāsūpaniṣatsu brahmavidyāyāṁ yogaśāstre śrīkṛṣṇārjunasaṁvāde
पुरुषोत्तमयोगो नाम पञ्चदशोऽध्यायः श्लोकः १०
puruṣottamayogo nāma pañcadaśo'dhyāyaḥ ślokaḥ 10

— ॐ —

उत्क्रामन्तं स्थितं वापि भुञ्जानं वा गुणान्वितम् ।
utkrāmantaṁ sthitaṁ vāpi bhuñjānaṁ vā guṇānvitam
विमूढा नानुपश्यन्ति पश्यन्ति ज्ञानचक्षुषः ॥१५-१०॥
vimūḍhā nānupaśyanti paśyanti jñānacakṣuṣaḥ (15-10)

The deluded do not know of this *Jīvātmā*—the soul—which enters and departs from the body, which is the indweller, which is the enjoyer of the sense-objects; but those endowed with the eye of wisdom, do perceive the indwelling soul alone to be the true reality in the scheme of things. (15.10)

—: Word-by-Word :—

उत्क्रामन्तम् utkrāmantam – departing; स्थितम् sthitam – residing; वा अपि vā api – or; भुञ्जानम् bhuñjānam – experiencing; वा api – or; गुणान्वितम् guṇānvitam – endowed with qualities; विमूढाः vimūḍhāḥ – the deluded; न na – do not; अनुपश्यन्ति anupaśyanti – perceive; पश्यन्ति paśyanti – see; ज्ञानचक्षुषः jñāna-cakṣuṣaḥ – those with the eye of knowledge.

—: Understanding The Verse :—

— ॐ योगवताराय नमः ॐ —

Having expounded in the preceding verses upon the nature of the जीवात्मा Jīvātmā, the embodied soul, as the one who migrates from body to body, presides over the senses, and "enjoys" the objects of the world through the medium of mind and matter, Shri Krishna anticipates our next inquiry: Who truly is able to discern this subtle Reality? And conversely, who fails to so perceive the Truth? The answer of course is the wise and the deluded fool.

— ॐ दयानिधानाय नमः ॐ —

The Lord here draws a sharp distinction between the ignorant and the wise. Though the जीवात्मा Jīvātmā continuously enters into various bodies, dwells within them as their inner ruler अन्तर्यामी (antaryāmin), and partakes of sensory experience, the deluded—those ensnared by māyā and blinded by the gunas—fail to perceive the indwelling soul.

Most people see just only these outer forms—the coming into the world of a being; and him growing up; and then subjected to disease, age, decay; and finally there's the inevitable perishing of the body—and they mistake these transient changes as happening to that being himself: that he was born, then he grew up, and then, alas, that being started shriveling up and one day died.

Nay, nay—nothing really happens to that being himself, and all the visible changes we perceive pertain just only to the outer sheath called the body. The indwelling Self, the Ātmā, remains ever the same—from birth to death he was the same and now he has journeyed on and he is still the same—except that he has added on a newer set of experiences in this life; and hopefully in some future birth all those experiences will add up and he will one day realize: In actuality I am one with the Divine.

But for most people, their vision stays clouded by ignorance अविद्या (avidyā), and they cannot pierce beyond the veils of material phenomena. By contrast, those who are endowed with the ज्ञान चक्षु jnāna-cakṣu—the eye of wisdom—behold the Self in its true light: as the unchanging reality.

— ॐ वेदाज्ञाय नमः ॐ —

The wise recognize that the soul, though associated with birth-death, pain-joys, remains ever-unborn, unchanging, and pure. Their vision is not confined to the gross physical frame but penetrates to the subtle essence—the indwelling consciousness that is the substratum of all experiences.

Thus, this verse serves as a clarion call, urging the aspirant to cultivate inner vision, to rise above the deceptions of sense and mind, and to perceive the soul as it truly is: untouched, eternal, ever-free—one within Krishna.

—: Key Sanskrit Terms :—

Let us explore the verse by focusing on the deeper implications of its key Sanskrit expressions:

— ॐ —

उत्क्रामन्तम् (utkrāmantam) – From the root क्राम krām (to step, move), उत्क्रामति utkrāmati means "to depart," especially at the time of death when the जीवात्मा jīvātman leaves the gross body.

It is not a movement in physical space, but a transition governed by subtle laws of कर्म karma and प्राण prāṇa.

— ॐ —

स्थितम् (sthitam) – "Remaining" or "residing."

It refers to the जीव jīva while it is embodied and dwelling in the body. This state of apparent stability is illusory, for the जीव jīva is ever in flux so long as ignorance अविद्या (avidyā) endures.

— ॐ —

भुञ्जानम् (bhuñjānam) – "Enjoying," derived from the root भुज् bhuj, meaning to partake, experience, or enjoy.

The term is laden with कर्म फल भोग karma-phala-bhoga—the experiencing of fruits of actions, both pleasant and painful. It points to the भोक्तृत्वम् bhoktṛtvam (the sense of being an enjoyer), which binds the soul.

— ॐ —

गुणान्वितम् (guṇānvitam) – "Endowed with the gunas."

The jīva appears as the enjoyer of the गुण gunas (sattva, rajas, tamas), though it is truly beyond them. This indicates the subtle identification with प्रकृति prakriti, the basis of phenomenal existence.

— ॐ —

विमूढाः (vimūḍhāḥ) – The "deluded," those whose intellects are clouded by अविद्या avidyā.

The prefix वि *vi-* intensifies the delusion: not merely ignorant, but deeply misled, unable to discern the real from the unreal.

— ॐ —

न अनुपश्यन्ति (na anupaśyanti) – न *Na* means "not," and अनुपश्यन्ति anupaśyanti means "do not perceive," but more precisely, "do not perceive with insight."

अनुपश्यन्ति Anupaśyanti implies seeing in accordance with तत्त्व tattva, the truth. The deluded see with the outer eye, not the eye of विवेक viveka (discrimination).

— ॐ —

पश्यन्ति (paśyanti) – "They see."

A verb of deep philosophical weight in Vedānta, पश्यन्ति paśyanti denotes not sensory vision but jnāna-dṛṣṭi, the eye of direct intuitive knowledge.

— ॐ —

ज्ञानचक्षुषः (jnāna-cakṣuṣaḥ) – "Those who have the eye of knowledge."

Here, चक्षु cakṣus symbolizes inner perception, प्रज्ञ-चक्षु prajñā-cakṣus—the ability to perceive the subtle, the unchanging Self amidst the changing appearances.

The word unites knowledge (jnāna) and sight, suggesting non-conceptual, luminous awareness.

—: *In Brief* :—

— ॐ श्रीकृष्णाय नमः ॐ —

In essence this verse unveils the stark contrast between ignorance and wisdom. The deluded, chained to superficial perception, imagine the Self to be born, to act, and to perish alongside the body.

They see the drama of embodiment—birth, growth, decay, and death—and erroneously superimpose these transitory attributes upon the Self, which in reality remains ever-aloof and immutable. Their eyes, though open, are blind to the truth.

By contrast, the wise—those endowed with discrimination (viveka) and illuminated by right knowledge—perceive the indwelling Self in all conditions: whether departing from one body, inhabiting another, or experiencing the diverse pleasures and pains of sensory life.

The wise realize that these changes are mere modifications of prakriti (material nature), while the Self remains untouched नित्य शुद्ध स्वतंत्र—nitya (eternal), śuddha (pure), and svatantra (self-existent).

Remember: In every phase of embodied existence, the same luminous One-Consciousness abides, unaltered by the movements of the gunas.

— ॐ श्रीरामाय नमः ॐ —

This verse impresses upon us the vital importance of inner purification and the cultivation of spiritual vision. Only when the eye of wisdom is opened does one see beyond the illusions of form and action, beholding the Self as it truly is—one within Braham, the ultimate Reality.

— ॐ केशवाय नमः ॐ —

Looking ahead, Shri Krishna now turns in the next verse to describe the characteristics of those rare souls who, through tireless striving and purity of heart, come to behold this truth directly. He also points out the deficiency of those who, despite effort, fail to perceive the Lord, indicating the subtle but crucial difference between mere endeavor and true realization.

Rejoice O mortal; see how Bhagwāna Shri Krishna's discourse to Arjuna keeps moving us ever deeper into the path of discernment and spiritual attainment.

— ॐ तत सत ॐ —

Before we move on, let us bow in reverence to this sacred verse. Write it by hand, reflect on its meaning, chant it aloud, make it your own.

— ॐ —

उत्क्रामन्तं स्थितं वापि भुञ्जानं वा गुणान्वितम् ।
utkrāmantaṁ sthitaṁ vāpi bhuñjānaṁ vā guṇānvitam
विमूढा नानुपश्यन्ति पश्यन्ति ज्ञानचक्षुषः ॥१५-१०॥
vimūḍhā nānupaśyanti paśyanti jñānacakṣuṣaḥ (15-10)

— ॐ —

उत्क्रामन्तं स्थितं वापि भुञ्जानं वा गुणान्वितम् ।
utkrāmantaṁ sthitaṁ vāpi bhuñjānaṁ vā guṇānvitam
विमूढा नानुपश्यन्ति पश्यन्ति ज्ञानचक्षुषः ॥ १५-१० ॥
vimūḍhā nānupaśyanti paśyanti jñānacakṣuṣaḥ (15-10)

ॐ तत्सदिति श्रीमद्भगवद्गीतासूपनिषत्सु ब्रह्मविद्यायां योगशास्त्रे श्रीकृष्णार्जुनसंवादे
om tatsaditi śrīmadbhagavadgītāsūpaniṣatsu brahmavidyāyāṁ yogaśāstre śrīkṛṣṇārjunasaṁvāde
पुरुषोत्तमयोगो नाम पञ्चदशोऽध्यायः श्लोकः १०
puruṣottamayogo nāma pañcadaśo'dhyāyaḥ ślokaḥ 10

Om-Tat-Sat—Om (Braham) is the sole Reality. In the Yogic Scripture on the Science-of-Braham, the Shrimada-Bhāgvada-Gītā Upanishad, we hereby conclude Shloka 10 of the Dialogue between Shrī Krishna and Arjuna entitled Purushottama-Yoga, Canto XV.

— ॐ वामनाय नमः ॐ —

Ashwattha—the Worldly-Tree

So turns the world upon thy limbs, O Tree of subtle forms—
Where deeds are sown and dreams are grown—
and every branch a whiplash storm.
Thou art the stage set for worldly play, wearing the veil of a jiva's face,
And all who act within thy boughs, forget their ID, their true place.
Here every joy becomes a bond, and sorrows dig us still more deep—
For both are thorny branches of this tree—where waking minds stay asleep.
O traveler of endless lives, do not love this entangling Tree-of-life—
It binds with songs and silken cords—it hates to set us free.
O mortal, climb not the Tree, but seek its very End—
Then rise through to become one in God—Him the rootless Flame.

ॐ गीता श्लोकः १५.११ – GĪTĀ VERSE 15.11

ॐ श्रीमद्भगवद्गीतासूपनिषत्सु ब्रह्मविद्यायां योगशास्त्रे श्रीकृष्णार्जुनसंवादे
om śrīmadbhagavadgītāsūpaniṣatsu brahmavidyāyāṁ yogaśāstre śrīkṛṣṇārjunasaṁvāde
पुरुषोत्तमयोगो नाम पञ्चदशोऽध्यायः श्लोकः ११
puruṣottamayogo nāma pañcadaśo'dhyāyaḥ ślokaḥ 11

— ॐ —

यतन्तो योगिनश्चैनं पश्यन्त्यात्मन्यवस्थितम् ।
yatanto yoginaścainaṁ paśyantyātmanyavasthitam
यतन्तोऽप्यकृतात्मानो नैनं पश्यन्त्यचेतसः ॥१५-११॥
yatanto'pyakṛtātmāno nainaṁ paśyantyacetasaḥ (15-11)

Yogīs—who strive—are able to directly perceive and realize the Self that is enshrined within their body; however those who are not self-controlled—being thoughtless—will not to see It in spite of trying. (15.11)

—: Word-by-Word :—

यतन्तः yatantaḥ – striving; योगिनः yoginaḥ – yogis; च ca – and; एनम् enam – this (soul); पश्यन्ति paśyanti – see; आत्मनि ātmani – within themselves; अवस्थितम् avasthitam – situated; यतन्तः api yatantaḥ api – though striving; अकृतात्मानः akṛtātmānaḥ – those with unrefined minds; न na – do not; एनम् enam – this (soul); पश्यन्ति paśyanti – see; अचेतसः acetasaḥ – the unintelligent.

—: Understanding The Verse :—

— ॐ श्रीकृष्णाय नमः ॐ —

Shri Krishna here reveals a timeless truth: mere striving is not sufficient for realization; it is the quality and purity of that striving which determines our success in the path.

The yogins—those steadfast seekers devoted to self-discipline and contemplation—through unwavering effort, discipline of mind, and inner purity, come to behold the indwelling Self, the Supreme Purusha seated within the heart.

These are aspirants whose inner vision does not get distracted by the flickering lights of worldly allurements; their gaze stays steadily turned inwards, and by the grace of intense striving यत्न (yatna) and mental clarity, they eventually come face to face with the Lord-God sitting within.

Conversely, there are those who, though they may engage in outer practices, lack true self-mastery. Their minds—still unrefined and clouded by attachments and the restlessness of desires—remain unfit to perceive the subtle truth of the Self.

Despite outward striving, their efforts are like seeds sown on barren ground, failing to blossom into the radiant flower of self realization.

— ॐ श्रीरामाय नमः ॐ —

This verse emphasizes the harsh truth: that spiritual success is not merely a function of effort, but of effort that's purified and distilled—effort guided by discrimination (viveka), purity of heart, and one-pointed devotion.

Remember: It is through these sacred qualities that the veils of ignorance get lifted and the radiant Self shines forth in an act of direct experience.

—: Key Sanskrit Terms :—

Let us unfold the inner meaning of the verse. Here, in the hush between terms, we may find the truest resonance—where the Sanskrit doesn't say, but sings; doesn't declare, but dreams.

— ॐ —

यतन्तः (yatantaḥ) – Derived from the root yat meaning "to strive" or "to make effort," this word emphasizes sustained inner endeavor.

Here, it implies not just outer effort, but intense, disciplined inward striving toward Self-realization आत्म ज्ञान (ātma-jnāna).

— ॐ —

योगिनः (yoginaḥ) – The yogīs are those who are united in mind and practice, engaged in ध्यान dhyāna, विवेक viveka, and वैराग्य vairāgya.

In this context, they are seekers of आत्मा Ātmā , not merely practitioners of postures or rituals. They walk the path of yoga in its highest sense—union with the Supreme-Self.

— ॐ —

एनं (enam) – "This" – referring to the जीवात्मा jīvātman, the indwelling Self, the subtle experiencer described in the preceding verses.

It is not a distant reality but intimately अवस्थितम् avasthitam—established within.

— ॐ —

पश्यन्ति (paśyanti) – "They see," but not with physical sight.

This is ज्ञान-दृष्टि jnāna-dṛṣṭi, inner perception through प्रज्ञा prajñā, born of purity and detachment. It connotes अपरोक्ष ज्ञान aparokṣa-jnāna—direct, immediate realization.

— ॐ —

आत्मनि अवस्थितम् (ātmany avasthitam) – "Established in the self."

A beautifully profound term. The Self is not an object to be attained elsewhere—it is ever-present within (ātmā), awaiting recognition. अवस्थितम् Avasthitam implies firm abidance—like oil in sesame seed, hidden yet intrinsic.

— ॐ —

अकृतात्मानः (akṛtātmānaḥ) – "Those whose selves are unprepared, undisciplined."

कृतात्मा Kṛta-ātmā is one who has purified and disciplined his inner instruments through शम दम उपारति śama, dama, uparati, and so forth. The अकृत आत्मा akṛta-ātmā is still enmeshed in externality and distracted by गुण विकार guna-vikāras.

— ॐ —

अचेतसः (acetasaḥ) – "Unconscious," or more subtly, "lacking inner awareness."

These are not intellectually dull, but rather inwardly inattentive—bereft of spiritual alertness. Their vision is turned outward; they do not perceive, even though they may look.

— ॐ —

न एनं पश्यन्ति (na enaṁ paśyanti) – "They do not see this."

Despite striving, the ज्ञान दृष्टिः jnāna-dṛṣṭi eludes them. The veil of माया māyā, sustained by impurity and ego, obstructs true vision.

—: *In Brief* :—

— ॐ श्रीकृष्णाय नमः ॐ —

In summation, this verse delineates with precision the path and the pitfall of the spiritual journey.

The yogins—those whose hearts are set unwaveringly upon God-realization—are depicted as those who, through disciplined effort यत्न (yatna) and self-mastery आत्म संयम (ātma-saṁyama), come to perceive the Lord dwelling within, the silent witness of all thoughts and actions.

Their striving is illumined by discrimination, and their vision is refined through the purification of mind and senses. In them, the inner eye opens, revealing the ever-present, all-encompassing Reality.

On the other hand, those whose striving is superficial, whose minds remain unpurified and scattered, fail to behold this supreme truth.

Their efforts, though outwardly similar, are devoid of the inner alchemy of self-transformation. Bound by heedlessness and the distractions of the external world, they remain strangers to the Self within.

— ॐ श्रीरामाय नमः ॐ —

This verse thus extols the necessity of inner purification and concentrated effort, making it clear that spiritual realization is not a casual attainment but the fruit of deep, sustained तपस tapas (austerity) and unwavering commitment.

Looking ahead, Shri Krishna now prepares to unveil His own transcendental nature—His supreme glory that surpasses even the brilliance of the sun, moon, and fire.

The question that arose earlier—how is it that these luminaries, which light up the universe, cannot illumine that Supreme Reality—is now addressed directly. The Lord begins to disclose His cosmic majesty, revealing the source of all illumination, and in doing so, opens the next profound section of the discourse, where His divine virtues and glories are laid bare for the seeker's contemplation.

— ॐ तत सत ॐ —

Before moving on, let us once more bow in deep reverence before this sacred verse of the Bhagavad-Gītā, an eternal beacon of wisdom that ceaselessly illumines the path of seekers. Engage with its form—inscribe it with your own hand, let your heart dwell upon its meaning, and raise your voice in its chanting—for within these syllables echoes the undying proclamation delivered millennia ago on the battlefield of Kurukshetra. These words, transmitted unchanged across the unbroken chain of generations, form a living bridge, linking us to that sanctified era when Bhagwāna Shri Krishna Himself walked this earth and bestowed this divine teaching. Through the luminous vibration of these sacred Sanskrit sounds, we are drawn nearer to His timeless presence, touching the very heartbeat of the Eternal..

— ॐ —

यतन्तो योगिनश्चैनं पश्यन्त्यात्मन्यवस्थितम् ।
yatanto yoginaścainaṁ paśyantyātmanyavasthitam
यतन्तोऽप्यकृतात्मानो नैनं पश्यन्त्यचेतसः ॥ १५-११ ॥
yatanto'pyakṛtātmāno nainaṁ paśyantyacetasaḥ (15-11)

— ॐ —

यतन्तो योगिनश्चैनं पश्यन्त्यात्मन्यवस्थितम् ।
yatanto yoginaścainaṁ paśyantyātmanyavasthitam
यतन्तोऽप्यकृतात्मानो नैनं पश्यन्त्यचेतसः ॥ १५-११ ॥
yatanto'pyakṛtātmāno nainaṁ paśyantyacetasaḥ (15-11)

ॐ तत्सदिति श्रीमद्भगवद्गीतासूपनिषत्सु ब्रह्मविद्यायां योगशास्त्रे श्रीकृष्णार्जुनसंवादे
om tatsaditi śrīmadbhagavadgītāsūpaniṣatsu brahmavidyāyāṁ yogaśāstre śrīkṛṣṇārjunasaṁvāde
पुरुषोत्तमयोगो नाम पञ्चदशोऽध्यायः श्लोकः ११
puruṣottamayogo nāma pañcadaśo'dhyāyaḥ ślokaḥ 11

Om-Tat-Sat—Om (Braham) is the sole Reality. In the Yogic Scripture on the Science-of-Braham, the Shrimada-Bhāgvada-Gītā Upanishad, we hereby conclude Shloka 11 of the Dialogue between Shrī Krishna and Arjuna entitled Purushottama-Yoga, Canto XV.

— ॐ वन्दे सूर्य शशाङ्क वह्निनयन वन्दे मुकुन्द प्रियम् ॐ —

When Words Refuse to Coddle, we must face the Uncomfortable Truth

How Bhagwāna Shri Krishna sings a quiet contrast here—
between those who see, and those who just gawk.
The Yogi—stripped-bare, inward-turned, tranquil-still—
pierces the veil,
not by force—but by ceasing!
And the others?
We chase, chant, churn, run.
We try—but never really truly.
Our heads are full of talk and wind,
Too glary that light for our eye—shrinks shut before the blazing truth.
Aye, no comfort this verse—a slashing thunder void of storm,
Lean bitter truth staring starkly in our face:
the Self is seen only when the 'Seeing' itself ceases.
This verse is flint-sharp, sorrow-wrought—
a dirge for the restless mind who drowns daily in the shallows,
while the DEEP keeps waiting within—unknown, unexplored.

—o—

The Flame Within the Flesh

O fool: Not in heaven. Not above clouds.
God sits right here—neath bone, right behind thy breath,
The Yogi turns inward—and there ends up having to bow,
For he finds a Fiery Flame burning therein—
Right where others forgot to look.

ॐ गीता श्लोकः १५.१२ – GĪTĀ VERSE 15.12

ॐ श्रीमद्भगवद्गीतासूपनिषत्सु ब्रह्मविद्यायां योगशास्त्रे श्रीकृष्णार्जुनसंवादे
om śrīmadbhagavadgītāsūpaniṣatsu brahmavidyāyāṁ yogaśāstre śrīkṛṣṇārjunasaṁvāde
पुरुषोत्तमयोगो नाम पञ्चदशोऽध्यायः श्लोकः १२
puruṣottamayogo nāma pañcadaśo'dhyāyaḥ ślokaḥ 12

— ॐ —

यदादित्यगतं तेजो जगद्भासयतेऽखिलम् ।
yadādityagataṁ tejo jagadbhāsayate'khilam
यच्चन्द्रमसि यच्चाग्नौ तत्तेजो विद्धि मामकम् ॥ १५-१२ ॥
yaccandramasi yaccāgnau tattejo viddhi māmakam (15-12)

The radiance in the sun which illumines the whole world, and which shines in the moon, and which gleams through the fire—know that Light to be Mine. (15.12)

—: *Word-by-Word* :—

यत् yat – that which; आदित्यगतम् āditya-gatam – in the sun; तेजः tejaḥ – light; जगत् jagat – the world; भासयते bhāsayate – illuminates; अखिलम् akhilam – the whole; यत् yat – that which; चन्द्रमसि candramasi – in the moon; यत् ca agnau – and that which is in fire; तत् tat – that; तेजः tejaḥ – light; विद्धि viddhi – know; मामकम् māmakam – as Mine.

—: *Understanding The Verse* :—

— ॐ श्रीकृष्णाय नमः ॐ —

In this luminous verse, Shri Krishna unfolds a vision of His immanence in the manifest cosmos, directing our gaze toward the fiery radiance which pervades all creation.

The Lord declares that the तेज tejas—the effulgence or divine brilliance manifest in the sun, moon, and fire—is not independent or self-existent but is a direct emanation of His own supreme essence.

These celestial bodies and elemental forces, though appearing as autonomous sources of light and life, are in truth but instruments through which the Supreme One is expressing His inexhaustible power and glory.

— ॐ श्रीरामाय नमः ॐ —

This verse serves as a corrective to the materialist's perception, which mistakes the sun, moon, and fire as ultimate sources of illumination.

Vedānta teaches that all phenomena, however splendid, are but transient reflections of Braham, the Supreme Reality, which alone is self-luminous and self-existent.

The jñānī, endowed with wisdom, perceives that behind the apparent multiplicity and diversity of luminous forms lies the singular and undivided Light of Īśvara, who both pervades and transcends His creation.

— ॐ जनानन्ददायकाय नमः ॐ —

By unveiling this subtle truth, the Lord invites us seekers to shift the centre of reverence from the outer brilliance of nature to the inner light of Consciousness, which illumines not only the world but also the very mind and intellect that behold it.

This teaching dissolves the veil of माया māyā, which beguiles the senses into perceiving the many as separate from the One, and reorients the aspirant toward the recognition of the Divine Presence in all forms of light and life.

—: Key Sanskrit Terms :—

Let us explore the verse; let us begin by meditating on its rich Sanskrit words:

— ॐ —

यद् आदित्यगतम् तेजः (yad ādityagataṁ tejaḥ) – "That light which is in the sun."

- आदित्य Āditya refers to the sun, the celestial eye of the cosmos, the great illuminator of all living beings.
- तेजः Tejas here signifies not merely physical luminosity but the शक्ति śakti—the intrinsic radiance, power, and consciousness that animates light itself.

— ॐ —

जगत् भासयते अखिलम् (jagat bhāsayate akhilam) – "Illumines the whole world."

- जगत् Jagat – "that which moves," the ever-changing world of name and form.
- भासयते Bhāsayate – "makes shine," or more deeply, "renders perceptible." This verb suggests the primal function of consciousness: to illumine all experience.
- अखिलम् Akhilam – "entirely, the entirety" indicating the universality of this divine light. There is nothing untouched by it.

— ॐ —

यत् चन्द्रमसि (yat candramasi) – "That which is in the moon."

- चन्द्र Candra (moon) symbolizes cool, nourishing light, the reflective principle, the rhythm of life and mind. The moon presides over the मनस् manas (mind), and this light is the seat of subtle perception and emotional balance.

— ॐ —

यत् च अग्नौ (yat ca agnau) – "That which is in the fire."

- अग्नि Agni is the terrestrial flame, both the literal fire and the inner fire of transformation, digestion जाठराग्नि (jāṭharāgni), and sacrifice यज्ञ (yajña). It is the purifying agent and messenger between realms.

— ॐ —

तत् तेजः विद्धि मामकम् (tat tejaḥ viddhi māmakam) – "Know that light to be Mine."

- तत् तेजः Tat tejaḥ – "That radiance," not distinct in each form, but a single luminous principle pervading all.

- विद्धि Viddhi – "Know" in an imperative tone: not simply as an intellectual concept, but as a deep realization (jnāna).

- मामकम् Māmakam – "Mine," belonging to Me—Shri Krishna as Iśvara, the Supreme Being. This pronoun is significant: the तेजः tejas is not independent; it is a reflection of the divine light of the Absolute.

—: In Brief :—

— ॐ श्रीकृष्णाय नमः ॐ —

This verse, in its luminous simplicity, unveils a profound secret: all that shines, all that glows, and all that warms in this cosmos is but a reflection of Braham's own splendor.

We Jivas, often ensnared by attachment to worldly objects, see them as substantial, significant, self-sustained. Yet, Bhagwāna Shri Krishna, in His infinite compassion, reveals here that the true source of their significance—their तेजः tejas, their very power to attract and sustain—is none other than He Himself.

Thus, the brilliance of the sun that sustains life, the cooling glow of the moon that soothes, and the vital warmth of fire that nourishes—all are but expressions of Bhagwāna Shri Krishna's inexhaustible radiance.

— ॐ श्रीरामाय नमः ॐ —

This teaching serves a dual purpose. It elevates our understanding, transforming the ordinary perception of nature into a sacred vision, wherein every beam of light becomes a pointer to the Divine. On the other hand, it also dissolves the illusion that material objects possess independent significance, gently severing the cords of attachment that bind the soul to संसार saṃsāra.

By recognizing the divine origin of all splendor, we gradually become disenchanted with the outer forms and get drawn inward—toward the eternal light of the Self.

— ॐ धर्मात्मने नमः ॐ —

This way Bhagwāna Shri Krishna prepares us for deeper realization. Having now revealed that His own तेजः tejas illumines the world, in the next verse He advances this teaching by showing how His energy sustains and vitalizes cosmic life itself.

The journey moves from perceiving the Lord's presence in the brilliance of light to understanding His intimate role as the very life-force that nurtures and upholds all existence. The discourse continues to deepen—drawing us ever closer to the heart of divine realization.

— ॐ तत सत ॐ —

Before we move on, let us bow in reverence to this sacred verse. Write it by hand, reflect on its meaning, chant it aloud, make it your own.

— ॐ —

यदादित्यगतं तेजो जगद्भासयतेऽखिलम् ।
yadādityagataṁ tejo jagadbhāsayate'khilam
यच्चन्द्रमसि यच्चाग्नौ तत्तेजो विद्धि मामकम् ॥ १५-१२ ॥
yaccandramasi yaccāgnau tattejo viddhi māmakam (15-12)

— ॐ —

यदादित्यगतं तेजो जगद्भासयतेऽखिलम् ।
yadādityagataṁ tejo jagadbhāsayate'khilam
यच्चन्द्रमसि यच्चाग्नौ तत्तेजो विद्धि मामकम् ॥ १५-१२ ॥
yaccandramasi yaccāgnau tattejo viddhi māmakam (15-12)

ॐ तत्सदिति श्रीमद्भगवद्गीतासूपनिषत्सु ब्रह्मविद्यायां योगशास्त्रे श्रीकृष्णार्जुनसंवादे
om tatsaditi śrīmadbhagavadgītāsūpaniṣatsu brahmavidyāyāṁ yogaśāstre śrīkṛṣṇārjunasaṁvāde
पुरुषोत्तमयोगो नाम पञ्चदशोऽध्यायः श्लोकः १२
puruṣottamayogo nāma pañcadaśo'dhyāyaḥ ślokaḥ 12

Om-Tat-Sat—Om (Braham) is the sole Reality. In the Yogic Scripture on the Science-of-Braham, the Shrimada-Bhāgvada-Gītā Upanishad, we hereby conclude Shloka 12 of the Dialogue between Shrī Krishna and Arjuna entitled Purushottama-Yoga, Canto XV.

ॐ गीता श्लोकः १५.१३ – GĪTĀ VERSE 15.13

ॐ श्रीमद्भगवद्गीतासूपनिषत्सु ब्रह्मविद्यायां योगशास्त्रे श्रीकृष्णार्जुनसंवादे
om śrīmadbhagavadgītāsūpaniṣatsu brahmavidyāyāṁ yogaśāstre śrīkṛṣṇārjunasaṁvāde
पुरुषोत्तमयोगो नाम पञ्चदशोऽध्यायः श्लोकः १३
puruṣottamayogo nāma pañcadaśo'dhyāyaḥ ślokaḥ 13

— ॐ —

गामाविश्य च भूतानि धारयाम्यहमोजसा ।
gāmāviśya ca bhūtāni dhārayāmyahamojasā
पुष्णामि चौषधीः सर्वाः सोमो भूत्वा रसात्मकः ॥ १५-१३ ॥
puṣṇāmi cauṣadhīḥ sarvāḥ somo bhūtvā rasātmakaḥ (15-13)

Entering the earth with my energy, it is I who support all creation through my vitality; and becoming the sap of moon, I nourish all herbs. (15.13)

—: Word-by-Word :—

गाम् gām – the earth; आविश्य āviśya – entering; च ca – and; भूतानि bhūtāni – beings; धारयामि dhārayāmi – I sustain; अहम् aham – I; ओजसा ojasā – with energy; पुष्णामि puṣṇāmi – nourish; च ca – and; औषधीः auṣadhīḥ – plants; सर्वाः sarvāḥ – all; सोमः somaḥ – as the moon; भूत्वा bhūtvā – becoming; रसात्मकः rasa-ātmakaḥ – full of sap.

—: Understanding The Verse :—

— ॐ श्रीकृष्णाय नमः ॐ —

In this lofty utterance, the Blessed Lord offers a focused exposition on His all-pervading essence, unfolding with serene clarity the perennial truths of सनातन धर्म Sanātana-Dharma. Here, the veil of mundane perception is gently lifted, revealing that the sustaining and nourishing forces of nature—so often regarded as independent or self-subsisting—are, in truth, none other than manifestations of Bhagwāna's own inexhaustible potency.

— ॐ श्रीरामाय नमः ॐ —

The verse evokes the imagery of the Lord pervading the very soil of the earth, silently upholding all living beings—whether they move or stand still—by the indwelling pulse of His शक्ति śakti.

This is not a mere poetic fancy but a philosophical revelation: the weight-bearing capacity of the earth, the vitality coursing through creatures, the very cohesion of elements—all these, though outwardly attributed to matter, are but reflections of सच्चिदानन्द ब्रह्म Sat-Cit-Ānanda Braham, whose manifest form is Shri Krishna Himself.

— ॐ यज्ञभुक्ताय नमः ॐ —

The heavens above, the blazing sun, the cooling moon, the boundless sky bejeweled with stars, the ten directions, the fathomless ocean, the revolving earth—all are upheld by that Supreme Principle, the eternal substratum of existence: ब्रह्म Braham.

The Lord declares that as the nectarine moon, He infuses vitality and nourishment into the realm of plants and herbs, sustaining the cycles of life and growth. Through this teaching, the veil of apparent autonomy is lifted, and all sustaining powers are shown to be but tributaries of the one Supreme Reservoir.

—: Key Sanskrit Terms :—

Let us illuminate the verse. Let the verse be a river and the Sanskrit its source—pure, high, cold with clarity. We do not need to bottle it; we only need to drink.

— ॐ —

गाम् आविश्य (gām āviśya) – "Entering the earth."

-गाम् Gām is the Vedic word for पृथ्वी pṛthvī—the earth, the nourishing mother of all beings.

- आविश्य Āviśya means "having entered," implying pervasion—not physical entry, but subtle immanence.

Bhagwāna does not merely stand apart from creation but pervades it from within as अन्तर्यामि antaryāmin.

— ॐ —

भूतानि धारयामि (bhūtāni dhārayāmi) – "I uphold all beings."

- भूतानि Bhūtāni refers to all created beings—all five-elemental forms from the highest gods to the smallest insect.

- धारयामि Dhārayāmi – "I sustain, support, uphold." This verb reflects ईश्वर Iśvara's role as धातृ dhātṛ—the cosmic sustainer.

— ॐ —

ओजसा (ojasā) – "With my energy."

- ओजस Ojas is not mere physical vigor, but the concentrated, vital essence of being—शक्ति śakti, the sustaining power of सत-चित sat-cit. It represents both subtle vitality and divine potency.

— ॐ —

पुष्णामि (puṣṇāmi) – "I nourish."

- From the root पुष् *puṣ*—to increase, to thrive. The Lord not only sustains beings but nourishes them from within, causing life to grow, mature, and flourish.

— ॐ —

औषधीः सर्वाः (auṣadhīḥ sarvāḥ) – "All herbs, plants, vegetation."

- औषधीः Auṣadhīḥ points to medicinal and nutritive plants—symbols of healing, sustenance, and life. It denotes the sacred interdependence between divine energy and earthly fertility.

— ॐ —

सोमः भूत्वा (somaḥ bhūtvā) – "Becoming the Moon (Soma)."

- सोम Soma is the lunar deity and sacred essence within plants. It is not merely the moon but the subtle रस rasa—the nourishing sap that circulates in flora, soma juice being sacred in Vedic ritual.

- It also symbolizes the mind, coolness, and intuitive wisdom—qualities necessary for spiritual nourishment.

— ॐ —

रसात्मकः (rasātmakaḥ) – "Of the nature of sap, essence, or vital fluid."

- रस Rasa is life-essence, taste, delight, and subtle energy. It also connotes the first product of digestion and the emotional sap of existence. Here, Bhagwāna is said to become that essence—He is the inner taste of life itself.

—: *In Brief* :—

— ॐ श्रीकृष्णाय नमः ॐ —

In this verse, by invoking the example of the earth and its perceived power to support all beings, the Lord reveals the deep metaphysical truth: that the sustaining force that appears inherent in the earth is, in reality, a fraction of His own divine potency.

Thus, not only the earth but every element that seems to uphold or nourish life does so solely through the infusion of His boundless energy.

The term रसात्मकः 'rasātmakaḥ' signifies the moon's essence as nectarine—full of the life-giving sap that nourishes all vegetation—yet this, too, is not autonomous but is a luminous extension of the Lord's own vibhūti.

— ॐ श्रीरामाय नमः ॐ —

Bhagwāna Shri Krishna graciously unveils the sublime vision that the entire cosmos—whether gross or subtle—is sustained by His अपरा प्रकृति aparā prakriti, His lower nature, which though termed 'lower,' remains inseparably united with Him.

He alone is the unseen Supporter, the Nourisher, the Illuminator—transcendent yet immanent in all.

Shri Krishna, the Supreme Refuge, the Lord-Master of the universe, silently upholds and sustains all beings and things in existence.

— ॐ नीलमणिवपुषे नमः ॐ —

Having thusly disclosed His hidden presence in the elemental forces of the universe, the Lord-God now turns, in the subsequent verse, to elucidate how even in the very act of digestion, He too is present—manifesting as the वैश्वानर vaiśvānara fire that digests food and assimilates nourishment—revealing yet another intimate aspect of His all-encompassing sovereignty.

— ॐ तत सत ॐ —

Before we move on, let us bow in reverence to this sacred verse. Write it by hand, reflect on its meaning, chant it aloud, make it your own.

— ॐ —

गामाविश्य च भूतानि धारयाम्यहमोजसा ।
gāmāviśya ca bhūtāni dhārayāmyahamojasā
पुष्णामि चौषधीः सर्वाः सोमो भूत्वा रसात्मकः ॥ १५-१३ ॥
puṣṇāmi cauṣadhīḥ sarvāḥ somo bhūtvā rasātmakaḥ (15-13)

— ॐ —

गामाविश्य च भूतानि धारयाम्यहमोजसा ।
gāmāviśya ca bhūtāni dhārayāmyahamojasā
पुष्णामि चौषधीः सर्वाः सोमो भूत्वा रसात्मकः ॥ १५-१३ ॥
puṣṇāmi cauṣadhīḥ sarvāḥ somo bhūtvā rasātmakaḥ (15-13)

ॐ तत्सदिति श्रीमद्भगवद्गीतासूपनिषत्सु ब्रह्मविद्यायां योगशास्त्रे श्रीकृष्णार्जुनसंवादे
om tatsaditi śrīmadbhagavadgītāsūpaniṣatsu brahmavidyāyāṁ yogaśāstre śrīkṛṣṇārjunasaṁvāde
पुरुषोत्तमयोगो नाम पञ्चदशोऽध्यायः श्लोकः १३
puruṣottamayogo nāma pañcadaśo'dhyāyaḥ ślokaḥ 13

Om-Tat-Sat—Om (Braham) is the sole Reality. In the Yogic Scripture on the Science-of-Braham, the Shrimada-Bhāgvada-Gītā Upanishad, we hereby conclude Shloka 13 of the Dialogue between Shrī Krishna and Arjuna entitled Purushottama-Yoga, Canto XV.

ॐ गीता श्लोकः १५.१४ – GĪTĀ VERSE 15.14

ॐ श्रीमद्भगवद्गीतासूपनिषत्सु ब्रह्मविद्यायां योगशास्त्रे श्रीकृष्णार्जुनसंवादे
om śrīmadbhagavadgītāsūpaniṣatsu brahmavidyāyāṁ yogaśāstre śrīkṛṣṇārjunasaṁvāde
पुरुषोत्तमयोगो नाम पञ्चदशोऽध्यायः श्लोकः १४
puruṣottamayogo nāma pañcadaśo'dhyāyaḥ ślokaḥ 14

— ॐ —

अहं वैश्वानरो भूत्वा प्राणिनां देहमाश्रितः ।
ahaṁ vaiśvānaro bhūtvā prāṇināṁ dehamāśritaḥ
प्राणापानसमायुक्तः पचाम्यन्नं चतुर्विधम् ॥ १५-१४॥
prāṇāpānasamāyuktaḥ pacāmyannaṁ caturvidham (15-14)

Taking the form of digestive fire (*Vaishvanara*), and united with the *Prāna* and *Apāna* breaths—it is I who digests and assimilates the four kinds of foods. (15.14)

—: *Word-by-Word* :—

अहम् aham – I; वैश्वानरः vaiśvānaraḥ – as the digestive fire; भूत्वा bhūtvā – becoming; प्राणिनाम् prāṇinām – of living beings; देहम् deham – in the body; आश्रितः āśritaḥ – residing; प्राणअपानसमायुक्तः prāṇa-apāna-samāyuktaḥ – united with the incoming and outgoing breaths; पचामि pacāmi – digest; अन्नम् annam – food; चतुर्विधम् caturvidham – of four kinds.

—: *Understanding The Verse* :—

— ॐ श्रीकृष्णाय नमः ॐ —

In this sacred verse Bhagwāna Shri Krishna, continuing His sublime exposition of divine immanence, reveals yet another facet of His intimate presence within all beings. Here, Krishna declares Himself as वैश्वानर Vaiśvānara—the universal digestive fire—enshrined in the bodies of all creatures. This sacred fire, harmonized with the vital currents of prāṇa and apāna, orchestrates the intricate process of digestion and assimilation, which sustains and nourishes embodied life.

— ॐ श्रीरामाय नमः ॐ —

The verse touches upon profound Vedic truths, affirming that not only is the Lord the cosmic supporter and nourisher—as earlier described—but He also dwells within, animating the subtle workings of the body.

The mention of वैश्वानर Vaiśvānara evokes the imagery of अग्नि Agni, the divine fire, which in the ancient श्रुति śruti is lauded as the consumer of offerings and the mediator between the mortal and the divine. Yet here, that same sacred fire is revealed to be none other than the Supreme Lord Himself, working ceaselessly within all beings to sustain them—to digest and transmute the fourfold types of food: those that are chewed, swallowed, licked, and sipped.

— ॐ दामोदराय नमः ॐ —

Through this revelation, the Lord imparts a vision of His omnipresence—not merely as a transcendent deity, but as the indwelling sustainer of the most ordinary and essential functions of life.

Thus, in this verse, the tapestry of Sanātana-Dharma is deepened, where even the act of nourishment becomes a sacrament, hallowed by the presence of the Divine. This śloka expresses Shri Krishna's immanence even in the internal functions of life like digestion.

—: *Key Sanskrit Terms* :—

Let us dwell upon the key Sanskrit terms to unravel the delicate strands of meaning woven into this श्लोक śloka. Each term is rich with philosophical and symbolic resonance:

— ॐ —

अहं वैश्वानरः भूत्वा (ahaṁ vaiśvānaraḥ bhūtvā) – "I, having become Vaiśvānara."

- अहम Aham – The Divine Self, speaking through Krishna as the Cosmic Being ईश्वर (Iśvara).

- वैश्वानर Vaiśvānara – Literally the Cosmic-Being, and it's also the universal fire, known as जाठराग्नि jāṭharāgni—the fire which digests .

Etymologically, वैश्वानर Vaiśvānara = विश्व viśva (Cosmos) + नर nara (Being) – which may be represented as the energy present in all beings. In Chāndogya Upaniṣad वैश्वानर Vaiśvānara is identified with the cosmic being and as representing the digestive power in individual beings and the light of the world in the macrocosm.

— ॐ —

प्राणिनां देहम् आश्रितः (prāṇinām deham āśritaḥ) – "Residing in the bodies of all living beings."

- प्राणिनां Prāṇinām – All those endowed with प्राण prāṇa, the vital life-force; all sentient beings.

- देहम् आश्रितः Deham āśritaḥ – "Dwelling within the body," suggesting immanence. The Lord abides within the individual body क्षेत्र (kṣetra) as its silent but essential sustainer.

— ॐ —

प्राणापानसमायुक्तः (prāṇāpāna-samāyuktaḥ) – "United with prāṇa and apāna."

- प्राण Prāṇa – The upward-moving vital energy, governing inhalation and upward functions.

- अपान Apāna – The downward-moving energy, governing exhalation and elimination.

- समायुक्तः Samāyuktaḥ – United with, coordinated. The Divine is not merely an observer but the inner orchestrator of physiological balance.

— ॐ —

पचामि (pacāmi) – "I digest."

- From पच *'pac'* – to cook, to digest, to transform. Here, the Supreme says I am the agency behind digestion, transforming अन्न anna (food) into रस rasa, ओजस् ojas, and प्राण life-force.

— ॐ —

अन्नं चतुर्विधम् (annaṁ caturvidham) – "The four kinds of food."

- Traditionally, these are:
- भक्ष्य Bhakṣya – foods that are chewed (solids),
- भोज्य Bhojya – foods swallowed without chewing (like soft foods),
- लेह्य Lehya – food that are licked (like pastes),
- चोस्य Cūṣya – food which are sipped (liquids).

This division symbolizes all forms of intake, whether gross or subtle.

—: *In Brief* :—

— ॐ श्रीकृष्णाय नमः ॐ —

In this verse, Shri Krishna solemnly unveils His form as वैश्वानर Vaiśvānara—the digestive fire that abides in the hearts of all beings.

This fire, though unseen, is the very force that digests and assimilates food, ensuring the sustenance of the body.

The Lord's identification with Vaiśvānara reminds us that no process, however mundane it may seem, operates independently of His supreme will and energy.

— ॐ श्रीरामाय नमः ॐ —

The vital airs—prāṇa and apāna—play their indispensable roles, directing the inward and outward flow of life's currents, working in unison with the digestive fire. Thus, the Lord, by uniting with these vital forces, governs the entire cycle of nourishment and vitality, without which embodied life would wither.

— ॐ यज्वने नमः ॐ —

The mention of the "four kinds of food"—भक्ष्य भोज्य पेय लेह bhakṣya, bhojya, peya, and leha—encompasses the full range of sustenance required by embodied beings, underscoring that all forms of nourishment are sanctified by His divine presence and power. Every meal, every act of sustenance, is thus seen as a यज्ञ yajña—a sacred offering in which the Lord Himself is both the giver and the receiver.

— ॐ विश्वमूर्तये नमः ॐ —

Having now expounded His roles as the supporter, nourisher, and digester—the unseen foundation of all life—Shri Krishna turns, in the forthcoming verse, to the ultimate declaration: that He alone is the supreme object of knowledge, the knower, and the goal of all wisdom. Thus, the teaching gracefully transitions from the realm of bodily sustenance to the supreme purpose of life—the realization of the Divine as the sole reality worth knowing and attaining.

— ॐ तत सत ॐ —

Before moving on, let us once more bow in deep reverence before this sacred verse of the Bhagavad-Gītā, an eternal beacon of wisdom that ceaselessly illumines the path of seekers. Engage with its form—inscribe it with your own hand, let your heart dwell upon its meaning, and raise your voice in its chanting—for within these syllables echoes the undying proclamation delivered millennia ago on the battlefield of Kurukshetra. These words, transmitted unchanged across the unbroken chain of generations, form a living bridge, linking us to that sanctified era when Bhagwāna Shri Krishna Himself walked this earth and bestowed this divine teaching. Through the luminous vibration of these sacred Sanskrit sounds, we are drawn nearer to His timeless presence, touching the very heartbeat of the Eternal..

— ॐ —

अहं वैश्वानरो भूत्वा प्राणिनां देहमाश्रितः ।
ahaṁ vaiśvānaro bhūtvā prāṇināṁ dehamāśritaḥ
प्राणापानसमायुक्तः पचाम्यन्नं चतुर्विधम् ॥१५-१४॥
prāṇāpānasamāyuktaḥ pacāmyannaṁ caturvidham (15-14)

— ॐ —

अहं वैश्वानरो भूत्वा प्राणिनां देहमाश्रितः ।
aham vaiśvānaro bhūtvā prāṇinām dehamāśritaḥ
प्राणापानसमायुक्तः पचाम्यन्नं चतुर्विधम् ॥ १५-१४ ॥
prāṇāpānasamāyuktaḥ pacāmyannam caturvidham (15-14)

ॐ तत्सदिति श्रीमद्भगवद्गीतासूपनिषत्सु ब्रह्मविद्यायां योगशास्त्रे श्रीकृष्णार्जुनसंवादे
om tatsaditi śrīmadbhagavadgītāsūpaniṣatsu brahmavidyāyāṁ yogaśāstre śrīkṛṣṇārjunasaṁvāde
पुरुषोत्तमयोगो नाम पञ्चदशोऽध्यायः श्लोकः १४
puruṣottamayogo nāma pañcadaśo'dhyāyaḥ ślokaḥ 14

Om-Tat-Sat—Om (Braham) is the sole Reality. In the Yogic Scripture on the Science-of-Braham, the Shrimada-Bhāgvada-Gītā Upanishad, we hereby conclude Shloka 14 of the Dialogue between Shrī Krishna and Arjuna entitled Purushottama-Yoga, Canto XV.

— ॐ दण्डकारण्य पुण्यकृते नमः ॐ —

Krishna, Whose Breath Makes the Sap to Stir

He comes not wrapped in thunder's cry nor strides through air with sword,
But enters humbly as the sap, and speaks without a word.
Within the tender shoot He flows, within the bud He sways,
And every herb that heals or blooms does echo back His praise.
The moon shines upon the herbs, but it's Krishna—the reason behind tastes;
The soil dost hold—but He the drive: Why seedlings break through soil,
to climb upwards in glee.
O gardener of inner fields, thou need'st not seek afar—
The Lord is leaf, the Lord is root, and the Lord is all you are.
And to touch a sapling is to touch His grace—in sweet, incarnate shape.

The Eater Too is He

There's an actual eater—who shines unseen behind flesh and breath.
Perhaps it's a man you see feasting—but it is He who digests.
O mortal, remember the Vaishvānara: the fire in belly, the altar within flesh.
He receives every offering: grain, liquid, thought, seed.
Yet man thanks the meal, not the real mouth behind.
Ah, the quiet irony: that the fire is divine, the feast divine,
but the muncher? He stays blind, ungrateful, loud.
No hymn he says to the Fire within, and—
the Self stays forgotten behind full stomachs and empty prayers.

ॐ गीता श्लोकः १५.१५ – GĪTĀ VERSE 15.15

ॐ श्रीमद्भगवद्गीतासूपनिषत्सु ब्रह्मविद्यायां योगशास्त्रे श्रीकृष्णार्जुनसंवादे
om śrīmadbhagavadgītāsūpaniṣatsu brahmavidyāyāṁ yogaśāstre śrīkṛṣṇārjunasaṁvāde
पुरुषोत्तमयोगो नाम पञ्चदशोऽध्यायः श्लोकः १५
puruṣottamayogo nāma pañcadaśo'dhyāyaḥ ślokaḥ 15

— ॐ —

सर्वस्य चाहं हृदि सन्निविष्टो मत्तः स्मृतिर्ज्ञानमपोहनञ्च ।
sarvasya cāhaṁ hṛdi sanniviṣṭo mattaḥ smṛtirjñānamapohanañca
वेदैश्च सर्वैरहमेव वेद्यो वेदान्तकृद्वेदविदेव चाहम् ॥ १५-१५ ॥
vedaiśca sarvairahameva vedyo vedāntakṛdvedavideva cāham (15-15)

It is I who remains seated in the hearts of all—as their inner controller. From Me is the knowledge and memory—or their loss. I am that ultimate Purport which the Vedas declare should be known in life. I am the origin of the Vedas and Vedānta; and it's I who am their Knower. (15.15)

—: Word-by-Word :—

सर्वस्य sarvasya – of all; च ca – and; अहम् aham – I; हृदि hṛdi – in the heart; सन्निविष्टः sanniviṣṭaḥ – situated; मत्तः mattaḥ – from Me; स्मृतिः smṛtiḥ – memory; ज्ञानम् jñānam – knowledge; अपोहनम् ca – and forgetfulness; वेदैः ca vedaiḥ – by all the Vedas; सर्वैः sarvaiḥ – all; अहम् एव aham eva – I alone; वेद्यः vedyaḥ – to be known; वेदान्तकृत् vedānta-kṛt – the compiler of Vedanta; वेदवित् vedavit – the knower of the Vedas; एव ca aham – indeed I am.

—: Understanding The Verse :—

— ॐ श्रीकृष्णाय नमः ॐ —

This verse stands as a luminous beacon within the fifteenth chapter of the Bhagavad Gītā, offering a sublime synthesis of divine immanence and transcendence.

Having thus far unfolded the cosmic tree of creation—the ashvattha—and its entanglement with the embodied soul, the Blessed Lord now lifts our gaze beyond the veils of materiality and mental constructs to the very heart of Existence.

— ॐ आत्मरूपाय नमः ॐ —

Here, Shri Krishna reveals Himself as the indwelling witness (antar-yāmin), seated deep within the hearts of all beings. Not merely a passive presence, He is the animating force behind all movements of thought and memory, as well as their lapses and obscurations. In this manner, He affirms that both knowledge and its apparent opposite stem from His inexhaustible power, reminding us that even ignorance and forgetfulness are woven into the fabric of His cosmic play.

— ॐ कृष्णाय वासुदेवाय हरये परमात्मने - प्रणत क्लेश नाशाय गोविन्दाय नमो नमः ॐ —

In what was a rising crescendo, the Lord now declares Himself to be the ultimate purport of all Vedic inquiry—the goal to which every hymn and verse of the Vedas is directed. Krishna is not only the fountainhead of the Vedas and the Vedānta, but also their supreme Knower, beyond whom no greater truth stands.

Thus, in a single breath, Bhagwāna Shri Krishna is revealed as the source, the essence, and the culmination of all sacred knowledge—a vision at once humbling and exalting.

—: Key Sanskrit Terms :—

Let us first unfold the deeper nuances of the verse by focusing on its luminous Sanskrit terms:

— ॐ —

सर्वस्य च अहं हृदि सन्निविष्टः (sarvasya ca ahaṁ hṛdi sanniviṣṭaḥ) – "I am seated in the heart of all beings."

- सर्वस्य Sarvasya – "Of all," without exception—every being from the microbe to the creator.

- हृदि Hṛdi – "In the heart." Not the physical organ, but the spiritual center—the dahara ākāśa, the subtle space of consciousness.

- सन्निविष्टः Sanniviṣṭaḥ – "Deeply entered, well-seated." This denotes not mere presence, but immanence. The Lord dwells not as a distant witness, but as the indwelling Self अंतरयामी (antaryāmin).

— ॐ —

मत्तः स्मृतिः, ज्ञानम्, अपोहनं च (mattaḥ smṛtiḥ jnānam apohanaṁ ca) – "From Me come memory, knowledge, and their removal (forgetfulness)."

- स्मृतिः Smṛtiḥ – Memory, the power of retention.

- ज्ञानम् Jnānam – Knowledge, in its pure form—illumined understanding.

- अपोहनं Apohanaṁ – Removal or negation, the fading of impressions, also the capacity to forget.

These are not self-generated faculties but gifts of the Divine, functioning through the grace and presence of the Self.

— ॐ —

वेदैः च सर्वैः अहम् एव वेद्यः (vedaiś ca sarvaiḥ aham eva vedyaḥ) – "By all the Vedas, I alone am to be known."

- वेदः Vedaḥ – Sacred knowledge, that which reveals the eternal truth.

- वेद्यः Vedyaḥ – That which is to be known, the object and goal of knowledge.

All the varied paths and hymns of the Veda converge toward a singular recognition: the realization of Braham, the Supreme Self.

— ॐ —

वेदान्तकृत् (vedānta-kṛt) – "I am the author of Vedānta."

- वेदान्त Vedānta – The "end of the Vedas," both literally and philosophically: the culmination of scriptural revelation found in the Upaniṣads.

- कृत् Kṛt – Creator, originator. The Lord declares Himself to be the source of the highest wisdom.

— ॐ —

वेदवित् एव च अहम् (vedavit eva ca aham) – "I alone am the true knower of the Vedas."

- वेदवित् Vedavit – The one who truly knows the Veda—not merely in words or rituals, but in essence.

- अहम् Aham – An emphatic: "I alone am that Knower," affirming non-duality.

Even the understanding of the Veda arises only by the light of the Self who illumines the intellect.

—: *In Brief* :—

— ॐ श्रीकृष्णाय नमः ॐ —

In this resplendent verse, the Lord discloses His ineffable intimacy with all sentient beings. He dwells as the silent knower within every heart, animating the faculties of memory, cognition, and also the veiling power that obscures true knowledge.

These, which seem to arise autonomously within the embodied being, are shown here to be but waves on the ocean of His divine consciousness. Even error and oblivion, so often feared or despised, are thus sanctified as instruments in the grand unfolding of spiritual evolution.

— ॐ श्रीरामाय नमः ॐ —

The verse reaches its zenith in the Lord's declaration that He is both the seed and the summit of the Vedas.

The Vedas, those ancient rivers of wisdom, find their wellspring in Him, and their deepest truths circle back to His lotus feet. The Vedānta—culminating in the unitive realization of Braham—is revealed not as an abstract metaphysical system but as a radiant expression of His very being.

Moreover, the Lord, as the ultimate वेदवित् Veda-vit (Knower of the Vedas), alone possesses the complete vision of their inner and outer meanings, which no intellect, however sharpened, can fully grasp without His grace.

— ॐ भगवते नमः ॐ —

This verse gathers together the streams of earlier teachings, presenting a panoramic view in which all knowledge, all striving, and all spiritual pursuit find their fulfilment in the Lord Himself.

We are being gently yet firmly guided to understand that beyond every ritual, every recitation, and every intellectual pursuit, it is the living presence of Shri Krishna—the embodiment of sat-cit-ānanda Braham—that is to be known and realized.

— ॐ पितृभक्ताय नमः ॐ —

Having thus expounded the Lord's immanence within the soul and His transcendence as the Supreme Object of knowledge, the discourse now turns, in the subsequent verses, to a precise delineation of क्षर kshara (the perishable), अक्षर akshara (the imperishable), and पुरुषोत्तम Puruṣottama—the Supreme Person—bringing the chapter's teaching to its profound philosophical culmination.

— ॐ तत सत ॐ —

Before moving on, let us once more bow in deep reverence before this sacred verse of the Bhagavad-Gītā, an eternal beacon of wisdom that ceaselessly illumines the path of seekers. Engage with its form—inscribe it with your own hand, let your heart dwell upon its meaning, and raise your voice in its chanting—for within these syllables echoes the undying proclamation delivered millennia ago on the battlefield of Kurukshetra. These words, transmitted unchanged across the unbroken chain of generations, form a living bridge, linking us to that sanctified era when Bhagwāna Shri Krishna Himself walked this earth and bestowed this divine teaching. Through the luminous vibration of these sacred Sanskrit sounds, we are drawn nearer to His timeless presence, touching the very heartbeat of the Eternal..

— ॐ —

सर्वस्य चाहं हृदि सन्निविष्टो मत्तः स्मृतिर्ज्ञानमपोहनञ्च ।
sarvasya cāhaṁ hṛdi sanniviṣṭo mattaḥ smṛtirjñānamapohanañca
वेदैश्च सर्वैरहमेव वेद्यो वेदान्तकृद्वेदविदेव चाहम् ॥ १५-१५॥
vedaiśca sarvairahameva vedyo vedāntakṛdvedavideva cāham (15-15)

— ॐ —

सर्वस्य चाहं हृदि सन्निविष्टो मत्तः स्मृतिर्ज्ञानमपोहनञ्च ।
sarvasya cāhaṁ hṛdi sanniviṣṭo mattaḥ smṛtirjñānamapohanañca
वेदैश्च सर्वैरहमेव वेद्यो वेदान्तकृद्वेदविदेव चाहम् ॥ १५-१५ ॥
vedaiśca sarvairahameva vedyo vedāntakṛdvedavideva cāham (15-15)

ॐ तत्सदिति श्रीमद्भगवद्गीतासूपनिषत्सु ब्रह्मविद्यायां योगशास्त्रे श्रीकृष्णार्जुनसंवादे
om tatsaditi śrīmadbhagavadgītāsūpaniṣatsu brahmavidyāyāṁ yogaśāstre śrīkṛṣṇārjunasaṁvāde
पुरुषोत्तमयोगो नाम पञ्चदशोऽध्यायः श्लोकः १५
puruṣottamayogo nāma pañcadaśo'dhyāyaḥ ślokaḥ 15

Om-Tat-Sat—Om (Braham) is the sole Reality. In the Yogic Scripture on the Science-of-Braham, the Shrimada-Bhāgvada-Gītā Upanishad, we hereby conclude Shloka 15 of the Dialogue between Shrī Krishna and Arjuna entitled Purushottama-Yoga, Canto XV.

— ॐ पुण्योदयाय नमः ॐ —

We are He. He is we.

A fragment? Nay, not cleft nor cut, but a mirrored flame of whole—
The Lord in sport, sends Himself down—as each and every soul.
Not a severed shard, nor a lesser spark, but same secret bloom of Light,
Which enters form and dons a veil, and walks through days and nights.
The ansha अंश hasn't been cast out of Him, nor thrown lost on distant shores—
He bears the seal of Paramatma Himself, silent at its core.
Thus Jiva rises clothed in breath, alternating songs within his sighs—
A dew upon the tree of Time—which knows not how or why!

— o —

Aye, in Whose gaze the stars stay hung, it is He alone who dwells:
in every little atom, in every human, in every single creature.
Just only He—the one Flame seated in all chests,
closer than thought, older than breath.
He does not enter from anywhere—He is already there.
The Vedas rise from Him, and man quotes the Vedas—
But Him he conveniently forgets!
From Him come knowing and forgetting.
He gives memory to us, or takes it—
Yet He is remembered by no fools here.

ॐ गीता श्लोकः १५.१६ – GĪTĀ VERSE 15.16

ॐ श्रीमद्भगवद्गीतासूपनिषत्सु ब्रह्मविद्यायां योगशास्त्रे श्रीकृष्णार्जुनसंवादे
om śrīmadbhagavadgītāsūpaniṣatsu brahmavidyāyāṁ yogaśāstre śrīkṛṣṇārjunasaṁvāde
पुरुषोत्तमयोगो नाम पञ्चदशोऽध्यायः श्लोकः १६
puruṣottamayogo nāma pañcadaśo'dhyāyaḥ ślokaḥ 16

— ॐ —

द्वाविमौ पुरुषौ लोके क्षरश्चाक्षर एव च ।
dvāvimau puruṣau loke kṣaraścākṣara eva ca
क्षरः सर्वाणि भूतानि कूटस्थोऽक्षर उच्यते ॥१५-१६॥
kṣaraḥ sarvāṇi bhūtāni kūṭastho'kṣara ucyate (15-16)

Of the two in the world—the Perishable and the Imperishable—the body of beings is spoken of as the Perishable, and the indwelling *Jīvātmā* as the Imperishable. (15.16)

—: Word-by-Word :—

द्वौ dvau – two; इमौ imau – these; पुरुषौ puruṣau – beings; लोके loke – in the world; क्षरः kṣaraḥ – the perishable; च ca – and; अक्षरः akṣaraḥ – the imperishable; एव ca – indeed; क्षरः kṣaraḥ – the perishable; सर्वाणि sarvāṇi – all; भूतानि bhūtāni – beings; कूटस्थः kūṭasthaḥ – the unchanging; अक्षरः akṣaraḥ – the imperishable; उच्यते ucyate – is said to be.

—: Understanding The Verse :—

— ॐ श्रीकृष्णाय नमः ॐ —

In this pivotal verse, Bhagwāna Shri Krishna articulates a fundamental distinction at the heart of सनातन धर्म Sanātana-Dharma—the division of existence into two principal categories: the क्षर kshara (perishable) and the अक्षर akshara (imperishable).

This dichotomy is not merely a classification of objects, but a profound ontological revelation that unveils the essential nature of reality as perceived through the vision of Vedānta.

— ॐ श्रीरामाय नमः ॐ —

The क्षर kshara encompasses all that is mutable and transient, including the gross physical bodies of beings and the entire field of material existence. This is the realm of prakriti—where birth, decay, and death are inescapable, and all forms are subject to dissolution.

Here, the Lord refers specifically to the embodied self, whose identification with the physical and subtle bodies renders it part of the perishable order.

In contrast, the अक्षर akshara signifies that which remains untouched by change—the imperishable self जीवात्मा (jīvātman), which, though residing in the body, remains intrinsically pure, eternal, and beyond decay.

This subtle essence, the शुद्धस्वरूप śuddha-svarūpa, transcends the fluctuations of the phenomenal world and points towards the higher reality of spirit.

In unveiling this twofold division, Shri Krishna invites us to stay discriminating between the fleeting and the eternal, and to repose faith not in the shifting sands of worldly existence, but in the immutable truth—that is the soul's very essence.

— ॐ सर्वाविगुणवर्जिताय नमः ॐ —

This verse stands as a clarion call to discernment, urging the aspirant to look beyond the illusory play of forms and to anchor one's consciousness in the imperishable reality, which alone bestows true freedom and bliss.

—: Key Sanskrit Terms :—

This verse introduces an ontological distinction—two types of beings in the manifest world. Let us examine the key terms for their layered meanings:

— ॐ —

द्वौ इमौ पुरुषौ लोके (dvau imau purushau loke) – "These two purushas exist in the world."

द्वौ Dvau – "Two," a binary classification that sets the stage for a Vedāntic gradation of reality.

इमौ Imau – "These (two)," referring to that which is present and known in the empirical domain लोक (loka).

पुरुषौ Purushau – The word purusha signifies "the conscious principle," yet here used in two forms: the jīva and the kshara.

लोके Loke – "In the world" — denoting व्यवहारिक सत्य vyāvahārika satya, the empirical realm of multiplicity and experience.

— ॐ —

क्षरः च अक्षरः एव च (ksharaḥ ca aksharaḥ eva ca) – "There is the Perishable, and there is also the Imperishable."

क्षरः Ksharaḥ – That which decays, changes, or perishes. Derived from the root क्ष kṣ (to decline), it refers to all transient phenomena—bodies, forms, names, ideas, and even subtle bodies.

अक्षरः Aksharaḥ – The imperishable, that which is not subject to decay. Not absolute ब्रह्म Braham, but the जीवात्मा jīvātman in its essential form, untouched by birth and death.

The two are juxtaposed as संस्कारिक samsāric (क्षर kshara) and मुक्तिक muktic (अक्षर akshara) realities within the created world.

— ॐ —

क्षरः सर्वाणि भूतानि (ksharaḥ sarvāṇi bhūtāni) – "All beings are perishable."

सर्वाणि भूतानि Sarvāṇi bhūtāni – All living entities, born of the five elements—gross and subtle bodies alike. These are under the sway of prakriti and the three gunas, and thus bound to change and dissolution.

क्षरः Ksharaḥ here represents the field of becoming, the क्षेत्र kṣetra (field) described in Chapter 13.

— ॐ —

कूटस्थः अक्षरः उच्यते (kūṭasthaḥ aksharaḥ ucyate) – "The unchanging, stable one is called the Imperishable."

कूटस्थः Kūṭasthaḥ – Literally "standing like an anvil" कूट (kūṭa)—unmoving, unchanging, and unaffected. It refers to the witness Self, the jīvātman as the reflected consciousness, untouched by bodily decay.

अक्षरः Aksharaḥ – Again, imperishable—not in the absolute (pāramārthika) sense, but relatively so within creation.

This is the inner purusha, the देही dehī, who transmigrates, experiences, but remains unchanged in essence.

—: In Brief :—

— ॐ श्रीकृष्णाय नमः ॐ —

In this verse, Bhagwāna Shri Krishna has laid bare the essential truth of existence: that the cosmos and all beings therein are woven from two distinct threads—the perishable and the imperishable.

The क्षर kshara—the body composed of the five gross elements and the machinery of the subtle body with its senses, mind, and intellect—belongs to the realm of the insentient and is destined for dissolution. Though vibrant in appearance, its vitality is but a borrowed light, kindled by the presence of the indwelling Self.

The अक्षर akshara, the imperishable soul, is the very spark of consciousness that animates this inert frame. It is this soul, a fragment of the Divine, that sustains the body's functions; and when it departs, the body, deprived of its animating force, perishes swiftly, becoming lifeless matter. Thus, the soul is the true essence, while the body and its faculties are mere instruments.

— ॐ अयोध्याधिपतये नमः ॐ —

Shri Krishna's teaching here also subtly dismantles the illusion of separateness.

What we call "individuality" is but a fragmentary view imposed by attachment and the false notion of 'mineness.'

In truth, all bodies and their actions are inseparable from the greater tapestry of Nature प्रकृति (prakriti). They belong not to the self but to the cosmic order, and thus, all actions must be performed in the spirit of lokasaṅgraha—for the protection of Dharma, not for personal gain.

— ॐ दयासिन्धवे नमः ॐ —

The अक्षर akshara—the imperishable—is beyond all modifications, untouched by the vicissitudes of material nature. While Nature is जड jaḍa (insentient), the soul, as a luminous ray of the Supreme, is चेतन cetana (sentient), bearing within itself the reflection of the Divine.

— ॐ मुकुन्दाय नमः ॐ —

Having now distinguished the perishable and imperishable principles, Shri Krishna prepares to unveil, in the next verse, the transcendent reality that surpasses both—the पुरुषोत्तम Puruṣottama, the Supreme-Being who stands beyond both matter and soul, as their ultimate substratum and sovereign Lord.

Thusly, the teaching has moved towards its zenith, where we are invited to contemplate not only the distinction between body and soul but also to behold that Supreme Reality which's beyond all duality—which alone is worthy of our seeking.

— ॐ तत सत ॐ —

Before we move on, let us bow in reverence to this sacred verse—a timeless beacon of wisdom guiding seekers for ages. Write it by hand, reflect on its meaning, and chant it aloud, for these sounds alone carry the authenticity of that era. The world may have changed but the living vibration of these Sanskrit sounds still

remain as original as they were when Bhagwān Shri Krishna Himself walked the earth and imparted these teachings.

— ॐ —

द्वाविमौ पुरुषौ लोके क्षरश्चाक्षर एव च ।
dvāvimau puruṣau loke kṣaraścākṣara eva ca
क्षरः सर्वाणि भूतानि कूटस्थोऽक्षर उच्यते ॥ १५-१६ ॥
kṣaraḥ sarvāṇi bhūtāni kūṭastho'kṣara ucyate (15-16)

— ॐ —

द्वाविमौ पुरुषौ लोके क्षरश्चाक्षर एव च ।
dvāvimau puruṣau loke kṣaraścākṣara eva ca
क्षरः सर्वाणि भूतानि कूटस्थोऽक्षर उच्यते ॥ १५-१६ ॥
kṣaraḥ sarvāṇi bhūtāni kūṭastho'kṣara ucyate (15-16)

ॐ तत्सदिति श्रीमद्भगवद्गीतासूपनिषत्सु ब्रह्मविद्यायां योगशास्त्रे श्रीकृष्णार्जुनसंवादे
om tatsaditi śrīmadbhagavadgītāsūpaniṣatsu brahmavidyāyāṁ yogaśāstre śrīkṛṣṇārjunasaṁvāde
पुरुषोत्तमयोगो नाम पञ्चदशोऽध्यायः श्लोकः १६
puruṣottamayogo nāma pañcadaśo'dhyāyaḥ ślokaḥ 16

Om-Tat-Sat—Om (Braham) is the sole Reality. In the Yogic Scripture on the Science-of-Braham, the Shrimada-Bhāgvada-Gītā Upanishad, we hereby conclude Shloka 16 of the Dialogue between Shrī Krishna and Arjuna entitled Purushottama-Yoga, Canto XV.

— ॐ यज्ञेश्वराय नमः ॐ —

Mistake not this outer Robe—to be Man himself.
The cloth frays. The wearer does not.
But still we mourn.
—We weep for faded threads, for sleeves become torn—
while the Self stays smiling—unclothed, untouched.

— o —

O Mortal Remeber This:
The Jiva is the Lord at play, the Light that wears a fleshy Veil—
A spark which leapt into the dark—who's now dreaming this mortal tale.
He hides himself in flesh and thought, in sorrows, joys & plays—
Forgetting what he truly is—he meanders lost: through births, forms, names.
Yet never really is he marred or torn, nor broken by the game—
He simply dreams as a Self become lost—and suffers in this frame.
But then, one blessed day, awakening comes—
Not as a roar, nor a flash from heaven's dome,
Perhaps as a smile which softly dawns: "I've always been at Home."
Then ends the game not with a cry—but mirthful laughter from inside out.

ॐ गीता श्लोकः १५.१७ – GĪTĀ VERSE 15.17

ॐ श्रीमद्भगवद्गीतासूपनिषत्सु ब्रह्मविद्यायां योगशास्त्रे श्रीकृष्णार्जुनसंवादे
om śrīmadbhagavadgītāsūpaniṣatsu brahmavidyāyāṁ yogaśāstre śrīkṛṣṇārjunasaṁvāde
पुरुषोत्तमयोगो नाम पञ्चदशोऽध्यायः श्लोकः १७
puruṣottamayogo nāma pañcadaśo'dhyāyaḥ ślokaḥ 17

— ॐ —

उत्तमः पुरुषस्त्वन्यः परमात्मेत्युदाहृतः ।
uttamaḥ puruṣastvanyaḥ paramātmetyudāhṛtaḥ
यो लोकत्रयमाविश्य बिभर्त्यव्यय ईश्वरः ॥१५-१७॥
yo lokatrayamāviśya bibhartyavyaya īśvaraḥ (15-17)

Apart from these there is the great Being—known as the *Param-Ātmā*, the Supreme-Soul, the immutable Lord—who, pervading the three worlds, sustains everything. (15.17)

—: Word-by-Word :—

उत्तमः uttamaḥ – the supreme; पुरुषः puruṣaḥ – being; तु tu – however; अन्यः anyaḥ – another; परमात्मा parama-ātmā – the Supreme Self; इति iti – thus; उदाहृतः udāhṛtaḥ – is called; यः yaḥ – who; लोकत्रयम् loka-trayam – the three worlds; आविश्य āviśya – pervading; बिभर्ति bibharti – sustains; अव्ययः avyayaḥ – the imperishable; ईश्वरः īśvaraḥ – Lord.

—: Understanding The Verse :—

— ॐ श्रीकृष्णाय नमः ॐ —

Verse 15.17 of the Bhagavad Gītā stands as yet another luminous pinnacle in the exposition of the Puruṣottama-Vidyā—the supreme knowledge of the Ultimate Person.

Having unfolded the twofold nature of existence—the क्षर kshara (perishable) and the अक्षर akshara (imperishable)—Shri Krishna now elevates the teaching beyond both, revealing the existence of a higher reality, the uttamaḥ purushaḥ, the Supreme Self, who alone transcends and encompasses all.

— ॐ श्रीरामाय नमः ॐ —

This Supreme-Being, the Paramātman, is distinct from both the mutable forms of the material universe and the changeless individual self.

He is the immutable Sovereign, the eternal Lord who pervades the three worlds—भूः भुवः स्वः bhūḥ, bhuvaḥ, and svaḥ—sustaining all realms of existence with effortless majesty.

Though immanent in all, He remains forever untouched by the fluctuations of time and space, preserving His absolute nature amidst the ever-shifting currents of creation.

— ॐ श्रीकृष्णाय परमात्मने नमः ॐ —

In this verse the Lord unveils the ultimate metaphysical truth that while the जीवात्मा jīvātman (individual soul) and प्रकृति prakriti (material nature) hold their respective places in the cosmic order, it is the परमात्मा Paramātman—the Supreme Reality—who is the source, the sustainer, and the final refuge of all.

Thus, this verse illumines the grand hierarchy of existence, drawing the aspirant's vision toward that highest पुरुष Purusha, who is not merely a part of the cosmos but its transcendent ground and goal.

This verse introduces the notion of a third Purusha, distinct from both the changing world क्षर (ksharaḥ) and the changeless individual self अक्षर (aksharaḥ), revealing the पुरुषोत्तम Puruṣottama, the Supreme-Being.

—: Key Sanskrit Terms :—

Let us unfold the inner meaning of the verse. Sometimes, the Sanskrit doesn't explain—it evokes. A flicker. A gesture. A scent of something eternal rising through syllables barely spoken.

— ॐ —

उत्तमः पुरुषः (uttamaḥ purushaḥ) – "The Supreme Being."

- उत्तमः Uttamaḥ – From उत् *'ut'* (above, beyond) and तम *'tama'* (superlative) — the "highest," "transcendent," and "supreme."
- पुरुषः Purushaḥ – The Conscious Being, the Knower of all fields क्षेत्रज्ञ (kṣetrajña).

This पुरुष Purusha is not subject to decay क्षर (kshara) nor merely the static witness अक्षर (akshara), but is the source and support of both. He is the non-dual Absolute, appearing as both the immanent and transcendent.

— ॐ —

अन्यः (anyaḥ) – "Different," or "distinct."

- Signifying ontological transcendence: This Supreme Self is other than the mutable beings and even the immutable witness (who still appears as individualized jīva).
- It does not mean duality or separateness, but rather superiority in तत्त्व tattva (truth-nature). The Supreme cannot be circumscribed within the duality of क्षर kshara and अक्षर akshara.

— ॐ —

परमात्मा (paramātmā) – "The Supreme Self."
- परमात्मा Paramātmā is the absolute Self—निर्गुण निर्विकार निराकार nirguna, nirvikāra, nirākāra.
- It is not merely the जीवात्मा jīvātman that resides in the heart, but the Self of all selves, the one Reality behind the many reflections.

— ॐ —

उदाहृतः (udāhṛtaḥ) – "Is declared" or "is described (in śāstra)."
- Implies that this understanding is rooted in श्रुति śruti—that the पुरुषोत्तम Puruṣottama is affirmed by the Vedas and perceived by the sages.
- The term lends scriptural authority आगम प्रमाण (āgamika-pramāṇa) to the verse.

— ॐ —

यो लोकत्रयम् आविश्य (yo loka-trayam āviśya) – "Who, having entered the three worlds..."
- लोकत्रयम् Loka-trayam – The "three worlds": भूः भुवः स्वः Bhūr (earth), Bhuvaḥ (mid-region), Svaḥ (heaven), representing gross, subtle, and causal realms.
- आविश्य Āviśya – "Entering" or "pervading." The Lord is not aloof; He enters all realms as the indwelling presence all-pervaded.

— ॐ —

बिभर्ति (bibharti) – "Sustains," "upholds," or "supports."
- Signifies divine immanence—the पुरुषोत्तम Puruṣottama is the bearer of all, the support of प्रकृति prakriti, the one who animates and governs all phenomena.
- It reflects the Lord's role as धात्र, भरता dhātṛ and bhartā—the sustainer and nourisher.

— ॐ —

अव्यय ईश्वरः (avyaya īśvaraḥ) – "The Immutable Lord."

- अव्यय Avyaya – That which does not perish, diminish, or undergo decay.

- ईश्वरः Īśvaraḥ – The Supreme Lord, the sovereign ruler, not merely a cosmic administrator, but the self-luminous intelligence चित्त शक्ति (cit-śakti) that governs without being governed.

—: In Brief :—

— ॐ श्रीकृष्णाय नमः ॐ —

In this exalted verse, Bhagwāna Shri Krishna deepens the vision imparted in the preceding teachings by disclosing the supreme truth that surpasses both the अक्षर kshara and the अक्षर akshara.

The devas—be they ब्रह्मा Brahammā, रुद्र Rudra, or other celestial beings—though mighty and long-lived, are ultimately bound within the cycle of saṃsāra. Their forms, no matter how resplendent, are subject to dissolution, marking them as part of the perishable order.

— ॐ श्रीरामाय नमः ॐ —

The अक्षर akshara, the changeless soul, remains untouched by such decay, embodying the eternal witness of all transformations. Yet even this pure self, while imperishable, is still limited by its individuality and its identification as a fragment of the whole.

Above both prevails the Supreme Being, the Ocean of Consciousness—सत-चित-आनन्द ब्रह्म sat-cit-ānanda Braham—whose manifest form is none other than Shri Krishna Himself.

ब्रह्म Braham is the infinite substratum in which both conscious (cit) and unconscious (acit) principles repose. Known as Kūṭastha—the immovable, unchanging core—He is the silent center around which the dance of creation unfolds. As the repository and sovereign of all, He pervades and upholds the universe while remaining utterly transcendent.

— ॐ हरये परमात्मने नमः ॐ —

This verse thus leads the aspirant to contemplate the Supreme as that which is not merely the goal of liberation but the very source from which all arises and into which all returns.

The scriptures resound with this truth: He is the inexhaustible fount of all being, the silent Witness, and the ultimate Fulfillment of every seeker's quest.

Having established His supreme identity as the Puruṣottama—the Supreme Person, who is beyond both the fleeting and the eternal—the Lord prepares, in the next verse, to unveil the secret culmination of this teaching, declaring His own unique place within this cosmic vision and thus bringing the chapter to its grand spiritual climax.

— ॐ तत सत ॐ —

Before we move on, let us bow in reverence to this sacred verse. Write it by hand, reflect on its meaning, chant it aloud, make it your own.

— ॐ —

उत्तमः पुरुषस्त्वन्यः परमात्मेत्युदाहृतः ।
uttamaḥ puruṣastvanyaḥ paramātmetyudāhṛtaḥ
यो लोकत्रयमाविश्य बिभर्त्यव्यय ईश्वरः ॥१५-१७॥
yo lokatrayamāviśya bibhartyavyaya īśvaraḥ (15-17)

— ॐ —

उत्तमः पुरुषस्त्वन्यः परमात्मेत्युदाहृतः ।
uttamaḥ puruṣastvanyaḥ paramātmetyudāhṛtaḥ
यो लोकत्रयमाविश्य बिभर्त्यव्यय ईश्वरः ॥१५-१७॥
yo lokatrayamāviśya bibhartyavyaya īśvaraḥ (15-17)

ॐ तत्सदिति श्रीमद्भगवद्गीतासूपनिषत्सु ब्रह्मविद्यायां योगशास्त्रे श्रीकृष्णार्जुनसंवादे
om tatsaditi śrīmadbhagavadgītāsūpaniṣatsu brahmavidyāyāṁ yogaśāstre śrīkṛṣṇārjunasaṁvāde
पुरुषोत्तमयोगो नाम पञ्चदशोऽध्यायः श्लोकः १७
puruṣottamayogo nāma pañcadaśo'dhyāyaḥ ślokaḥ 17

Om-Tat-Sat—Om (Braham) is the sole Reality. In the Yogic Scripture on the Science-of-Braham, the Shrimada-Bhāgvada-Gītā Upanishad, we hereby conclude Shloka 17 of the Dialogue between Shrī Krishna and Arjuna entitled Purushottama-Yoga, Canto XV.

— ॐ पीतवाससे नमः ॐ —

The Hidden Sovereign Within

The mind doth rise, the senses dance, the body plays its part,
Yet all by Him are moved and held—that silent Witness within the heart.
He tasteth not the fruit of acts, though all through Him arise,
He stays untouched, unmoved, unbound—by this world which woos the eyes.
He is the Fire within the wood, the Life in silent seed,
He's the Flame that flickers not with wind, nor bends to mortal needs.
Though He partakes of sense's fare, His essence is never stirred—
Like the Space untouched by clouds below, or echo by the word.

— o —

But why weepest thou, O friend? And what is it thou celebrate today?
Do that, O soul, but first wake up and know: Thou art that Sovereign—
Who lives beyond both joy and wail—a Witness pure.

ॐ गीता श्लोकः १५.१८ – GĪTĀ VERSE 15.18

ॐ श्रीमद्भगवद्गीतासूपनिषत्सु ब्रह्मविद्यायां योगशास्त्रे श्रीकृष्णार्जुनसंवादे
om śrīmadbhagavadgītāsūpaniṣatsu brahmavidyāyāṁ yogaśāstre śrīkṛṣṇārjunasaṁvāde
पुरुषोत्तमयोगो नाम पञ्चदशोऽध्यायः श्लोकः १८
puruṣottamayogo nāma pañcadaśo'dhyāyaḥ ślokaḥ 18

— ॐ —

यस्मात्क्षरमतीतोऽहमक्षरादपि चोत्तमः ।
yasmātkṣaramatīto'hamakṣarādapi cottamaḥ
अतोऽस्मि लोके वेदे च प्रथितः पुरुषोत्तमः ॥१५-१८॥
ato'smi loke vede ca prathitaḥ puruṣottamaḥ (15-18)

I am beyond the *Kshetra* (the perishable body), and higher even to the *Kshetrajna* (the imperishable soul); so therefore, the Vedas and the world describe Me as *Purushottama*—the Supreme Being. (15.18)

—: *Word-by-Word* :—

यस्मात् yasmāt – because; क्षरम् kṣaram – the perishable; अतीतः atītaḥ – transcending; अहम् aham – I; अक्षरात् akṣarāt – than the imperishable; अपि api – even; च ca – and; उत्तमः uttamaḥ – superior; अतः ataḥ – therefore; अस्मि asmi – I am; लोके loke – in the world; वेदे ca vede – and in the Vedas; प्रथितः prathitaḥ – renowned; पुरुषोत्तमः puruṣottamaḥ – as the Supreme Person.

—: *Understanding The Verse* :—

— ॐ श्रीकृष्णाय नमः ॐ —

In this lofty shloka, Bhagwāna Shri Krishna unveils the culminating vision of the पुरुषोत्तम-तत्त्व Purushottama-Tattva, marking a profound conclusion to the philosophical ascent of the पुरुषोत्तम-योग Purushottama Yoga.

Having already delineated the twin categories of existence—the क्षर Kshara (the mutable, perishable realm of matter) and the अक्षर Akshara (the immutable, imperishable soul)—the Lord now reveals that He transcends both.

Here, Krishna solemnly declares that He is verily the Supreme-Being, the पुरुषोत्तम Purushottama, acknowledged not merely by human wisdom but affirmed by the timeless testimony of the Vedas and the sacred lore.

— ॐ श्रीरामाय नमः ॐ —

This verse, shimmering with metaphysical grandeur, reaffirms the Vedāntic vision: while प्रकृति Prakriti and जीव Jīva are vast and unfathomable in themselves, both find their ultimate root and highest purpose in the Paramātman, the Supreme Self.

Shri Krishna emphatically distinguishes Himself as not only the sustainer and inner ruler of the perishable cosmos and the imperishable soul but as the ultimate substratum beyond them both.

His transcendence is absolute, standing above both the transient and the eternal, binding the entire existential spectrum into the oneness of His supreme being.

— ॐ सत्यसंधाय नमः ॐ —

This verse is a sublime declaration of the Lord's supreme sovereignty, wherein He explicitly claims the epithet पुरुषोत्तम Purushottama, grounding it not in arbitrary assertion but in the deepest metaphysical truth as sung by the Vedic sages and echoed in all sanctified traditions.

—: *Key Sanskrit Terms* :—

This verse is Bhagwāna's explicit declaration of His supreme status as पुरुषोत्तम Puruṣottama, the Being beyond both the changing and the unchanging. Let us unfold the meaning of its central terms:

— ॐ —

यस्मात् क्षरम् अतीतः अहम् (yasmāt ksharam atītaḥ aham) – "Because I transcend the perishable."

यस्मात् Yasmāt – "Because," indicating the cause or reasoning behind the declaration.

क्षरम् Ksharam – The perishable world—everything subject to birth, growth, decay, and death.

अतीतः Atītaḥ – "I am beyond," not merely outside, but untouched, unaffected, transcending all change.

Bhagwāna is not bound by the field क्षेत्र (kṣetra), the body, mind, or world.

— ॐ —

अक्षरात् अपि च उत्तमः (akṣarāt api ca uttamaḥ) – "And I am higher even than the imperishable."

अक्षरात् Akṣarāt – From the imperishable, namely the जीवात्मा jīvātman, the immutable witness within the individual, which, though unaffected, remains distinct and individuated under अविद्या avidyā.

उत्तम Uttamaḥ – "Supreme," beyond even that, not merely in degree, but in ontological reality.

The अक्षर akshara remains witness to phenomena; but पुरुषोत्तम Puruṣottama is the source and substratum of even that witness.

— ॐ —

अतोऽस्मि लोके वेदे च प्रथितः (ato'smi loke vede ca prathitaḥ) – "Therefore, I am well-known in the world and in the Vedas."

अतोऽस्मि Ato'smi – "Thus I am" or "Therefore I am" (known as such).

लोके Loke – In the world of people and sages, among realized beings and seekers.

वेदे च Vede ca – And in the śāstra, especially the Upaniṣads, which consistently declare the पुरुषोत्तमः तत्त्व Puruṣottama tattva.

प्रथितः Prathitaḥ – "Renowned," "proclaimed," "widely known," both revealed in scripture and realized by sages.

— ॐ —

पुरुषोत्तमः (puruṣottamaḥ) – "The Supreme Purusha."

पुरुष Purusha – The conscious being, the Self.

उत्तम Uttamaḥ – The highest, transcending both क्षर kshara (perishable) and अक्षर akshara (imperishable).

पुरुषोत्तमः Puruṣottama is thus the non-dual Absolute परम-ब्रह्म (parama-brahma), beyond the dualities of change and stasis, beyond प्रकृति prakriti and जीव jīva, yet immanently supporting both.

—: *In Brief* :—

— ॐ श्रीकृष्णाय नमः ॐ —

In the luminous clarity of this verse, the mystery of the Lord's supreme status is laid bare. By employing the emphatic अहम् 'Aham'—I am the पुरुषोत्तम Purushottama—the Lord draws Arjuna's gaze toward the ultimate fountainhead of all existence.

Shri Krishna is not merely beyond the mutable क्षर Kshara—the ever-shifting play of matter—nor merely loftier than the immutable अक्षर Akshara—the luminous but finite soul. Rather, He is the source and sovereign of both, untouched by their respective limitations and dualities.

While the क्षेत्रज्ञ Kṣetrajña (knower of the field) enjoys the immortality of spirit, even it remains within the ambit of Prakriti, whereas the Lord alone stands as the transcendent governor, unsullied by matter, beyond the modes of nature, and resplendent in His own innate fullness.

— ॐ सेतुकृते नमः ॐ —

This proclamation, crowned by the declaration that the Vedas themselves bear witness to His supreme stature, firmly situates the Lord as the ultimate axis of all spiritual pursuit and realization.

The subtle play of terms—यस्मात् 'Yasmāt' (because) and अतः 'Ataḥ' (therefore)—weaves a logical thread, sealing the conclusion that it is by virtue of this transcendence that He rightfully bears the title of Purushottama, the Supreme-Being.

— ॐ श्रीरामाय नमः ॐ —

Having established this majestic truth, the Lord, in the verses that follow, turns to illuminate the transformative power of such knowledge. He extols the glories of the one who recognizes and realizes Him as पुरुषोत्तम Purushottama, outlining the marks of true wisdom and the supreme merit accruing to such realization.

Thus, the discourse moves from metaphysical declaration to the fruits of spiritual recognition, guiding us aspirants ever closer to liberation's highest summit.

— ॐ तत सत ॐ —

Before we move on, let us bow in reverence to this sacred verse. Write it by hand, reflect on its meaning, chant it aloud, make it your own.

— ॐ —

यस्मात्क्षरमतीतोऽहमक्षरादपि चोत्तमः ।
yasmātkṣaramatīto'hamakṣarādapi cottamaḥ
अतोऽस्मि लोके वेदे च प्रथितः पुरुषोत्तमः ॥१५-१८॥
ato'smi loke vede ca prathitaḥ puruṣottamaḥ (15-18)

— ॐ —

यस्मात्क्षरमतीतोऽहमक्षरादपि चोत्तमः ।
yasmātkṣaramatīto'hamakṣarādapi cottamaḥ
अतोऽस्मि लोके वेदे च प्रथितः पुरुषोत्तमः ॥१५-१८॥
ato'smi loke vede ca prathitaḥ puruṣottamaḥ (15-18)

ॐ तत्सदिति श्रीमद्भगवद्गीतासूपनिषत्सु ब्रह्मविद्यायां योगशास्त्रे श्रीकृष्णार्जुनसंवादे
om tatsaditi śrīmadbhagavadgītāsūpaniṣatsu brahmavidyāyāṁ yogaśāstre śrīkṛṣṇārjunasaṁvāde
पुरुषोत्तमयोगो नाम पञ्चदशोऽध्यायः श्लोकः १८
puruṣottamayogo nāma pañcadaśo'dhyāyaḥ ślokaḥ 18

Om-Tat-Sat—Om (Braham) is the sole Reality. In the Yogic Scripture on the Science-of-Braham, the Shrimada-Bhāgvada-Gītā Upanishad, we hereby conclude Shloka 18 of the Dialogue between Shrī Krishna and Arjuna entitled Purushottama-Yoga, Canto XV.

ॐ गीता श्लोकः १५.१९ – GĪTĀ VERSE 15.19

ॐ श्रीमद्भगवद्गीतासूपनिषत्सु ब्रह्मविद्यायां योगशास्त्रे श्रीकृष्णार्जुनसंवादे
om śrīmadbhagavadgītāsūpaniṣatsu brahmavidyāyāṁ yogaśāstre śrīkṛṣṇārjunasaṁvāde
पुरुषोत्तमयोगो नाम पञ्चदशोऽध्यायः श्लोकः १९
puruṣottamayogo nāma pañcadaśo'dhyāyaḥ ślokaḥ 19

— ॐ —

यो मामेवमसम्मूढो जानाति पुरुषोत्तमम् ।
yo māmevamasammūḍho jānāti puruṣottamam
स सर्वविद्भजति मां सर्वभावेन भारत ॥१५-१९॥
sa sarvavidbhajati māṁ sarvabhāvena bhārata (15-19)

Being thus undeluded, he who truly knows Me as the *Purushottama*, he truly knows it all, O Bhārata; and he naturally venerates Me in every respect.
(15.19)

—: Word-by-Word :—

यः yaḥ – who; माम् mām – Me; एवम् evam – thus; असम्मूढः asammūḍhaḥ – undeluded; जानाति jānāti – knows; पुरुषोत्तमम् puruṣottamam – as the Supreme Person; सः saḥ – he; सर्ववित् sarvavit – all-knowing; भजति bhajati – worships; माम् mām – Me; सर्वभावेन sarvabhāvena – with all his being; भारत bhārata – O Bharata.

—: Understanding The Verse :—

— ॐ श्रीकृष्णाय नमः ॐ —

In this culminating verse of the पुरुषोत्तम दर्शन Purushottama Darśana, Shri Krishna draws the grand teaching to its apex, imparting the fruit of the supreme knowledge revealed thus far.

With serene authority, Krishna proclaims that the one who, freed from delusion, realizes Him as the Purushottama—the Supreme Person—attains a state of true omniscience.

Such a knower does not merely gather fragmented bits of knowledge but perceives the integral essence of all that exists, beholding in Krishna the wellspring and final aim of every phenomenon, both material and spiritual.

— ॐ श्रीरामाय नमः ॐ —

This verse underscores that realization of the Supreme-Being is not a matter of dry metaphysics but a profound inner transformation that leads inevitably to total devotion.

Knowing the Lord in truth compels the heart to surrender fully, embracing Him with undivided love and veneration. The Lord thus teaches that true wisdom culminates in bhakti—the spontaneous and whole-hearted worship of the Supreme, where knowledge and devotion merge inseparably.

— ॐ अनन्तगुण गम्भीराय नमः ॐ —

Through this verse, the Gītā illumines that the path of discernment (jnāna) and the path of devotion (bhakti) are not opposed but converge upon the same sublime summit: the living realization of the Purushottama, who alone is to be known, and who alone is worthy of total adoration.

—: Key Sanskrit Terms :—

This verse is a luminous summation—declaring the fruit of knowing Puruṣottama as taught in the previous verses. Each term is richly expressive:

— ॐ —

यो माम् एवम् असम्मूढः जानाति (yo mām evam asammūḍhaḥ jānāti) — "He who, being undeluded, thus knows Me..."

यो Yo – "He who," the qualified knower, the seeker who attains direct realization.

माम् Mām – "Me," referring to Bhagwāna in His supreme aspect as Puruṣottama.

एवम् Evam – "Thus," indicating in this very manner—as declared in the preceding verse (15.18).

असम्मूढः Asammūḍhaḥ – "Undeluded," one who is free from moha (delusion), avidyā (ignorance), and adhyāsa (superimposition).

जानाति Jānāti – "Knows," not merely intellectually शास्त्र ज्ञान (śāstra-jnāna), but as अपारोक्ष अनुभव aparokṣa-anubhava—direct, unshakable realization of the non-dual Self.

— ॐ —

पुरुषोत्तमम् (puruṣottamam) — "The Supreme Purusha."

This refers to the non-dual Absolute, beyond both क्षर kshara (perishable) and अक्षर akshara (imperishable).

To know the पुरुषोत्तम Puruṣottama is to realize that: "I am not merely the embodied being, nor only the witnessing self, but the very source and substratum of both—limitless, changeless, indivisible."

— ॐ —

सः सर्ववित् (saḥ sarvavit) — "He is the knower of all."

सर्ववित् Sarvavit – The one who knows everything—not in terms of informational omniscience, but as one who has known the substratum of all, by which all else is known.

As the Muṇḍaka Upaniṣad says:

"Yena sarvam idam vijñātaṁ bhavati" "By knowing That, all this becomes known." Such a person sees all names and forms as manifestations of the one Reality, the पुरुषोत्तम Puruṣottama.

— ॐ —

भजति मां सर्वभावेन (bhajati māṁ sarvabhāvena) — "He worships Me with all his being."

भजति Bhajati – Not mere ritual worship. In its deepest sense, भज bhaj means "to unite with," "to adore with love and knowledge," or "to abide in constant remembrance and surrender."

सर्वभावेन Sarvabhāvena – "With all dispositions," "in every way," "with the totality of his being."

This is the fruit of knowledge ज्ञान (jnāna): devotion arises naturally. The knower of puruṣottama does not see the Lord as other, but loves and worships as an expression of oneness.

— ॐ —

भारत (bhārata) "O descendant of Bharata" – An affectionate address to Arjuna, but also a reminder of the dhārmic heritage Arjuna bears, which seeks truth through inner clarity and unwavering surrender.

—: *In Brief* :—

— ॐ श्रीकृष्णाय नमः ॐ —

In this verse, Bhagwāna Shri Krishna sets forth the crowning vision of the Gītā's teaching. The one who truly discerns Him as the पुरुषोत्तम Purushottama—higher than both the perishable and the imperishable—is lifted beyond all lesser attachments and finds rest in the all-encompassing truth.

Such a knower, even if devoid of formal learning, is endowed with the highest wisdom, for to know the Supreme-Being is to know the very essence from which all things arise and into which all return.

— ॐ श्रीसीतामनोरमाय नमः ॐ —

In this perfected knowledge, the heart is purified of all worldly inclinations. The devotee's inner and outer life becomes one seamless act of worship, where every thought, word, and deed flows naturally toward the Lord.

This is not mere ritual homage, but a surrender of the entire being—a devotion characterized by अनन्य-भक्ति ananya-bhakti, unswerving and unfragmented.

— ॐ श्रीनिधये नमः ॐ —

The subtle point is beautifully clear: so long as any attachment to the ephemeral world lingers, true worship remains partial. But when realization dawns that the Lord transcends both the mutable body and even the immutable soul, the devotee's entire nature is magnetized toward Him alone.

— ॐ सत्यमूर्तये नमः ॐ —

Verse 15.19 completes the exposition of the Supreme-Being, tracing the soul's ascent from the field of the perishable, through the imperishable soul, to the ultimate reality of God Himself.

In perfect accord with the method of अरुन्धति-दर्शन-न्याय Arundhatī-darśana-nyāya—guiding the seeker from the gross to the subtle—the Lord has now revealed the highest aim.

In the next verse, the discourse pivots to unveil the profound purpose behind this entire revelation, drawing together the threads of knowledge and devotion into their ultimate fruit.

— ॐ तत सत ॐ —

Before moving on, let us once more bow in deep reverence before this sacred verse of the Bhagavad-Gītā, an eternal beacon of wisdom that ceaselessly illumines the path of seekers. Engage with its form—inscribe it with your own hand, let your heart dwell upon its meaning, and raise your voice in its chanting—for within these syllables echoes the undying proclamation delivered millennia ago on the battlefield of Kurukshetra. These words, transmitted unchanged across the unbroken chain of generations, form a living bridge, linking us to that sanctified era when Bhagwāna Shri Krishna Himself walked this earth and bestowed this divine teaching. Through the luminous vibration of these sacred Sanskrit sounds, we are drawn nearer to His timeless presence, touching the very heartbeat of the Eternal..

— ॐ —

यो मामेवमसम्मूढो जानाति पुरुषोत्तमम् ।
yo māmevamasammūḍho jānāti puruṣottamam
स सर्वविद्भजति मां सर्वभावेन भारत ॥१५-१९॥
sa sarvavidbhajati māṁ sarvabhāvena bhārata (15-19)

— ॐ —

यो मामेवमसम्मूढो जानाति पुरुषोत्तमम् ।
yo māmevamasammūḍho jānāti puruṣottamam
स सर्वविद्भजति मां सर्वभावेन भारत ॥ १५-१९ ॥
sa sarvavidbhajati māṁ sarvabhāvena bhārata (15-19)

ॐ तत्सदिति श्रीमद्भगवद्गीतासूपनिषत्सु ब्रह्मविद्यायां योगशास्त्रे श्रीकृष्णार्जुनसंवादे
om tatsaditi śrīmadbhagavadgītāsūpaniṣatsu brahmavidyāyāṁ yogaśāstre śrīkṛṣṇārjunasaṁvāde
पुरुषोत्तमयोगो नाम पञ्चदशोऽध्यायः श्लोकः १९
puruṣottamayogo nāma pañcadaśo'dhyāyaḥ ślokaḥ 19

Om-Tat-Sat—Om (Braham) is the sole Reality. In the Yogic Scripture on the Science-of-Braham, the Shrimada-Bhāgvada-Gītā Upanishad, we hereby conclude Shloka 19 of the Dialogue between Shrī Krishna and Arjuna entitled Purushottama-Yoga, Canto XV.

— ॐ सच्चिदानन्दविग्रहाय नमः ॐ —

Here's the last flaming cry of the Canto—
the voice that breaks all names—
not to destroy—but to reveal.
A thunder-cloaked Hush, crowned with fire—
To awaken the world which likes to count dust,
but stays forgetful of the Source from where dust and counting has emerged.

— o —

"O Mortal, know:
To know That-One, Purushottam – पुरुषोत्तम - is to know it all."
Know not the parts—but the very Pulse.
Know by Becoming—not just through thoughts,
No more question. No more walk. No more seeker. No more sought.
The knower becomes the knowing and the Known—
And he perforce bows,
Not out of duty—but because Recognition itself so compels.

ॐ गीता श्लोकः १५.२० – GĪTĀ VERSE 15.20

ॐ श्रीमद्भगवद्गीतासूपनिषत्सु ब्रह्मविद्यायां योगशास्त्रे श्रीकृष्णार्जुनसंवादे
om śrīmadbhagavadgītāsūpaniṣatsu brahmavidyāyām̐ yogaśāstre śrīkṛṣṇārjunasam̐vāde
पुरुषोत्तमयोगो नाम पञ्चदशोऽध्यायः श्लोकः २०
puruṣottamayogo nāma pañcadaśo'dhyāyaḥ ślokaḥ 20

— ॐ —

इति गुह्यतमं शास्त्रमिदमुक्तं मयानघ ।
iti guhyatamam̐ śāstramidamuktam̐ mayānagha
एतद्बुद्ध्वा बुद्धिमान्स्यात्कृतकृत्यश्च भारत ॥ १५-२० ॥
etadbuddhvā buddhimānsyātkṛtakṛtyaśca bhārata (15-20)

Thus has this most esoteric of doctrines been expounded by me, O sinless one. Knowing this, one becomes wise; and accomplished thereby are all the duties of his life, O Bhārata." (15.20)

—: Word-by-Word :—

इति iti – thus; गुह्यतमम् guhyatamam – most secret; शास्त्रम् śāstram – scripture; इदम् idam – this; उक्तम् uktam – has been spoken; मया mayā – by Me; अनघ anagha – O sinless one; एतत् etat – this; बुद्ध्वा budd hvā – having understood; बुद्धिमान् buddhimān – wise; स्यात् syāt – becomes; कृतकृत्यः kṛta-kṛtyaḥ – accomplished in all duties; च ca – and; भारत bhārata – O Bharata.

—: Understanding The Verse :—

— ॐ श्रीकृष्णाय नमः ॐ —

Verse 15.20 stands as the solemn epilogue to the sublime discourse of the पुरुषोत्तम दर्शन Purushottama Darśana Yoga, bringing to closure the profound revelation of the Supreme Self.

In this verse, Shri Krishna, the compassionate teacher of all beings, affirms that the doctrine He has imparted is not a mere assemblage of philosophical tenets but is the deepest and most esoteric wisdom—a गुह्यतम शास्त्र guhyatama śāstra—the supreme secret of all spiritual knowledge.

— ॐ श्रीरामाय नमः ॐ —

Here, the Lord impresses upon Arjuna, and indeed upon all seekers, the unparalleled sanctity of this teaching. Unlike ordinary doctrines that cater to the superficial mind, this wisdom penetrates to the very root of existence, guiding the soul to its ultimate fulfillment.

This esoteric secret, transcendent and luminous, reveals the nature of the Supreme-Being, who stands above both the perishable world of matter and the imperishable soul. To know this truth is to be established in the fullness of wisdom; to assimilate it is to achieve the supreme goal of human existence.

— ॐ श्रीकान्ताय नमः ॐ —

This verse functions as both a benediction and a charge: it extols the transformative power of the knowledge just imparted and enjoins the sincere seeker to embrace it with reverence and resolve.

The साधक sādhaka who receives and internalizes this teaching is no longer bound by the ordinary duties and aims of life but fulfils them all through the realized vision of the Divine.

—: Key Sanskrit Terms :—

Let us unfold the meaning and nuance within the central terms of this verse. Each word, each syllable, is a footfall in dust long settled. We walk softly through this verse, letting its Sanskrit speak in the quiet we create by listening.

— ॐ —

इति गुह्यतमं शास्त्रम् (iti guhyatamaṁ śāstram) —"Thus this most secret doctrine..."

इति Iti – "Thus," referring to the culmination of the teaching from verses 15.1 to 15.19.

गुह्यतमं Guhyatamam – Superlative of guhya (secret, hidden): meaning "most secret," "most subtle," or "most esoteric."

This teaching is not hidden due to concealment, but because it is incomprehensible to the impure mind, grasped only by the subtle intellect purified by विवेक viveka (discrimination), वैराग्य vairāgya (dispassion), and श्रद्धा śraddhā (reverence).

शास्त्रम् Śāstram – "Doctrine" or "scriptural teaching," not just theoretical, but authentic original शास्त्र śāstra as शासनात् त्रायते śāsanāt trayate—that which disciplines शासनात् śāsanāt and thereby liberates त्रायते trayate.

— ॐ —

इदमुक्तं मया अनघ (idam uktaṁ mayā anagha) — "This has been spoken by Me, O sinless one."

इदमुक्तं Idam uktaṁ – "This has been declared," a divine affirmation of the authority and completeness of the teaching.

मया Mayā – By Me, Bhagwāna, the Puruṣottama Himself—the speaker is not a teacher bound by time but the eternal knower and source of the Veda. (मया Mayā should not to be confused with the word माया Māyā).

अनघ Anagha – "O sinless one" – a gentle and reverent address to Arjuna, recognizing his receptivity and purity (अदोष-योग्य a-dosha-yogya), a necessary qualification (अधिकार adhikāra) to receive such truth.

— ॐ —

एतद्बुद्ध्वा (etadbuddhvā) — "Having known this..."

From बुद्धि buddhi (discriminative knowledge), बुद्धवा buddhvā implies direct and mature understanding—not just hearing or believing, but deep assimilation through श्रवण śravaṇa, मनन manana, निदिध्यासन nididhyāsana (hearing, reflection, contemplation).

— ॐ —

बुद्धिमान् स्यात् (buddhimān syāt) —"One becomes wise."

Buddhimān – "A knower," "a man of discernment."

Not one who merely has learning शास्त्र ज्ञान (śāstra-jnāna), but one whose intellect is illumined by Self-knowledge—who sees the One Reality pervading the many.

— ॐ —

कृतकृत्यः च (kṛtakṛtyaḥ ca) —"And accomplished in all duties."

कृतकृत्यः Kṛta-kṛtyaḥ – "One who has done what is to be done."

This is a key Vedāntic expression: the one who has fulfilled the highest purpose of human life—realization of his Self, the Ātmā as non-different from Braham.

No further karma remains binding for such a person. He has crossed the sea of becoming भव सागर (bhava-sāgara).

— ॐ —

भारत (bhārata) "O Bhārata" – Again, a loving invocation of Arjuna's noble lineage, but also an echo to the seeker:

"O heir of Dharma, O seeker of Truth, receive this supreme wisdom and become free."

—: In Brief :—

— ॐ श्रीकृष्णाय नमः ॐ —

In this concluding pronouncement, Shri Krishna seals the majestic teaching of the Purushottama Darśana with both finality and grace.

The Lord's words—"इति गुह्यतमं शास्त्रमिदमुक्तं iti guhyatamaṃ śāstram-idamuktaṁ"—underscore that this doctrine is the crown jewel of spiritual instruction, encapsulating the essence of all the Vedas and the deepest mysteries of existence.

This secret has been expounded in its totality, revealing the full arc of divine reality: from the mutable realm of क्षर kshara, through the immutable अक्षर akshara, and culminating in the transcendence of the पुरुषोत्तम Purushottama Himself.

— ॐ श्रीरामाय नमः ॐ —

Shri Krishna assures that whoever, with a purified heart and undistracted mind, receives and contemplates this knowledge becomes सर्ववित् sarvavit, बुद्धिमान buddhimān—truly wise.

Such a one not only attains intellectual clarity but embodies the highest purpose of life कृतकृत्यः (kṛtakṛtyaḥ), fulfilling all that is to be accomplished in human existence. This is the consummation of both action and knowledge: the harmony of jnāna and karma through the prism of realized devotion.

— ॐ वेदविद्याविशारदाय नमः ॐ —

This verse gracefully concludes the chapter by affirming that the ultimate aim of life is the realization of the Supreme Self, through which all duties, obligations, and spiritual quests are brought to their rightful consummation.

Having delivered this sacred teaching, the Lord prepares to turn the discourse toward its next unfolding in the next Chapter—and where the implications of such wisdom continue to ripple through the ensuing chapters, guiding us ever deeper into the heart of divine realization.

— ॐ तत सत ॐ —

Before moving on, let us once more bow in deep reverence before this sacred verse of the Bhagavad-Gītā, an eternal beacon of wisdom that ceaselessly illumines the path of seekers. Engage with its form—inscribe it with your own hand, let your heart dwell upon its meaning, and raise your voice in its chanting—for within these syllables echoes the undying proclamation delivered millennia ago on the battlefield of Kurukshetra. These words, transmitted unchanged across the unbroken chain of generations, form a living bridge, linking us to that sanctified era when Bhagwāna Shri Krishna Himself walked this earth and bestowed this divine teaching. Through the luminous vibration of these sacred Sanskrit sounds, we are drawn nearer to His timeless presence, touching the very heartbeat of the Eternal..

— ॐ —

इति गुह्यतमं शास्त्रमिदमुक्तं मयानघ ।
iti guhyatamaṁ śāstramidamuktaṁ mayānagha
एतद्बुद्ध्वा बुद्धिमान्स्यात्कृतकृत्यश्च भारत ॥१५-२०॥
etadbuddhvā buddhimānsyātkṛtakṛtyaśca bhārata (15-20)

— ॐ —

इति गुह्यतमं शास्त्रमिदमुक्तं मयानघ ।
iti guhyatamaṁ śāstramidamuktaṁ mayānagha
एतद्बुद्ध्वा बुद्धिमान्स्यात्कृतकृत्यश्च भारत ॥१५-२०॥
etadbuddhvā buddhimānsyātkṛtakṛtyaśca bhārata (15-20)

ॐ तत्सदिति श्रीमद्भगवद्गीतासूपनिषत्सु ब्रह्मविद्यायां योगशास्त्रे श्रीकृष्णार्जुनसंवादे
om tatsaditi śrīmadbhagavadgītāsūpaniṣatsu brahmavidyāyāṁ yogaśāstre śrīkṛṣṇārjunasaṁvāde
पुरुषोत्तमयोगो नाम पञ्चदशोऽध्यायः श्लोकः २०
puruṣottamayogo nāma pañcadaśo'dhyāyaḥ ślokaḥ 20

Om-Tat-Sat—Om (Braham) is the sole Reality. In the Yogic Scripture on the Science-of-Braham, the Shrimada-Bhāgvada-Gītā Upanishad, we hereby conclude Shloka 20 of the Dialogue between Shrī Krishna and Arjuna entitled Purushottama-Yoga, Canto XV.

— ॐ दशरथात्मजाय नमः ॐ —

The One Who Dwells Within All Hearts

In chambers veiled behind mind's bright veils,
There sits the Lord, upon Heart's still throne.
Not far, nor near—rather nearer than thy breath, nearer than thy very own "I",
He reigns within—yet stays unseen and never gets known from outside.

— o —

He needeth not a temple wrought by hands,
For lo, the soul itself is His abode.
He listens not with ears, yet He hears each and every thought.
Aye, Krishna is the Antaryamin, silent and sublime,
Who knows all thy dreams—before they dare to climb.

— o —

"Thus has the most-esoteric of doctrines been expounded"—spoke the Flame
Most-esoteric—yet made most-simple by the voice of Krishna.
And yet...the world spins still, and Jivas keep spinning in it—
chained by their own thoughts, drunk on acting out inanities—
For they have given up lucid reasoning, have abandoned the Luculent Gita.
No riddle here. No tangled word. No secret scroll.
The Self is so plain—but stunned on the head, the fool never looks Gita's way.

ॐ Chapter Fifteen Recap

The fifteenth chapter of the Bhagavad Gītā, titled Purushottama Yoga, presents a sublime and compact vision of reality, weaving together cosmology, ontology, and the supreme goal of human life.

This chapter serves as a microcosm of the entire Gītā, distilling its vast teachings into a meditation on the nature of existence and the supreme truth that transcends it.

— ॐ —

The chapter begins (**verses 1 through 6**) with a vivid allegory of the universe, likened to the imperishable Ashvattha tree, whose roots extend upwards and branches downward.

Bhagwāna Shri Krishna instructs the seeker to sever attachment to this world-tree with the weapon of detachment, guiding the soul beyond the entanglements of saṃsāra toward the imperishable abode, parama dhāma.

— ॐ —

In **verses 7 through 11**, we see the Lord reveal the nature of the jīva, the individual soul, as an eternal part of Himself—but who stays caught in the cycle of birth and death due to bondages forged with material nature. He describes the soul's journey through embodiment, its experience of the senses, and its departure at death, illustrating the deep entwinement of the soul with the field of matter.

— ॐ —

Verses 12 through 15 disclose the divine immanence of the Lord: we discover that Krishna pervades the cosmos as the sustaining principle—manifest in the light of the sun and moon, in the nourishing power of the earth, and as the fire of digestion within all beings. It is revealed that He alone is the prabhu—the indwelling Lord—of all knowledge, the object of the Vedas, and the knower of all.

— ॐ —

In **verses 16 and 17**, a pivotal metaphysical distinction is drawn between the kshara purusha (the perishable being) and the akshara purusha (the imperishable self), with Shri Krishna declaring Himself as the uttama purusha—the Supreme-Being—who transcends both. Here, the ontology of the Gītā reaches its zenith, affirming that while both matter and soul are vast and ancient, the Lord stands beyond them as the ultimate reality.

— ॐ —

Verse 18 reinforces this supreme position: Krishna asserts that because He is beyond both the mutable and immutable, He is rightly declared in the Vedas and in the world to be Purushottama, the Supreme-Being.

— ॐ —

In **verse 19**, we are told that the one who, undeluded, truly realizes Krishna as the Purushottama, becomes wise in the highest sense and naturally worships the Lord with all his being. This is the fruit of supreme knowledge—complete devotion and the fulfillment of life's ultimate purpose.

— ॐ —

Finally, in **verse 20**, the Lord proclaims that this doctrine is the most esoteric of all teachings. Having grasped it, the seeker attains true wisdom and fulfills every duty of life, achieving spiritual perfection.

— ॐ —

One of the shortest Gitā chapters, Chapter 15 spans a wide panorama: it reveals the structure of existence through the metaphor of the cosmic tree, describes the soul's journey through the realms of matter, affirms the Lord's immanence and transcendence, and culminates in the revelation of the Purushottama—the Supreme Person—who is the source, sustainer, and our ultimate goal.

The next chapter, Chapter 16: Daivasura Sampad Vibhaga Yoga, will transition from metaphysical exposition to an ethical analysis of human nature. It delineates the divine and demoniac qualities (daivī and āsurī), offering practical guidance for cultivating virtue and avoiding the pitfalls that obstruct the path to liberation. Thus, the Gītā continues its graceful movement between the heights of philosophy and the grounding wisdom of righteous living.

ॐ तत्सदिति श्रीमद्भगवद्गीतासूपनिषत्सु ब्रह्मविद्यायां योगशास्त्रे श्रीकृष्णार्जुनसंवादे
om tatsaditi śrīmadbhagavadgītāsūpaniṣatsu brahmavidyāyāṁ yogaśāstre śrīkṛṣṇārjunasaṁvāde
पुरुषोत्तमयोगो नाम पञ्चदशोऽध्यायः ॥
puruṣottamayogo nāma pañcadaśo'dhyāyaḥ .

Om-Tat-Sat—Om (Braham) is the sole Reality. In this Yogic Scripture on the Science of Brahama—the Shrimada-Bhāgvada-Gītā Upanishad—hereby ends the dialogue between Shrī Krishna and Arjuna entitled: Purushottama Yoga, Canto XV.

[O Seeker, we thank thee for reading thus far. This has been a brief commentary and lots still remains unsaid. Rāma-willing, our exhaustive commentary will become available in 2026. This is our init endeavor and surely it's full of many faults which we fully own—and we pray thou shalt take it in thy heart to pardon us. Bhagavad-Gitā is a celestial stream and any human touch, however well-meaning, only sullies it some. We hope to be forgiven by Bhagwana Shri Krishna for daring to torture this sublime text of His, which has no parallels anywhere—never will.]

ॐ ॐ ॐ ॐ ॐ ॐ ॐ ॐ ॐ ॐ ॐ ॐ ॐ ॐ ॐ ॐ ॐ ॐ

ॐ गीतामाहात्म्यम् GĪTĀ-MĀHĀTMYAM

[Verses on the glory and import of the Bhagavad-Gītā]

— ॐ —

गीताशास्त्रमिदं पुण्यं यः पठेत्प्रयतः पुमान् ।
gītāśāstramidaṁ puṇyaṁ yaḥ paṭhetprayataḥ pumān ,
विष्णोः पदमवाप्नोति भयशोकादिवर्जितः ॥
viṣṇoḥ padamavāpnoti bhayaśokādivarjitaḥ .

One who diligently studies this Bhagavad-Gītā—the bestower of all virtues—with firm devotion and a regulated mind—verily attains Vaikuntha—the holy abode of Māhā-Vishnu—and he stands freed of all the fears and sorrows of this mundane world.

— ॐ —

गीताध्ययनशीलस्य प्राणायामपरस्य च ।
gītādhyayanaśīlasya prāṇāyāmaparasya ca ,
नैव सन्ति हि पापानि पूर्वजन्मकृतानि च ॥
naiva santi hi pāpāni pūrvajanmakṛtāni ca .

One who performs Prāṇāyāms and studies the Bhagavad-Gītā regularly and sincerely—all his sins melt away, even those from all prior lives.

— ॐ —

मलनिर्मोचनं पुंसां जलस्नानं दिने दिने ।
malanirmocanaṁ puṁsāṁ jalasnānaṁ dine dine ,
सकृद्गीताम्भसि स्नानं संसारमलनाशनम् ॥
sakṛdgītāmbhasi snānaṁ saṁsāramalanāśanam .

A daily bath removes external bodily taints, but a single bath in the sacred waters of Bhagavad-Gītā is enough to remove all the taints of this Saṁsāra—this polluting worldly existence of joys, sorrows, births, and deaths.

— ॐ —

गीता सुगीता कर्तव्या किमन्यैः शास्त्रविस्तरैः ।
gītā sugītā kartavyā kimanyaiḥ śāstravistaraiḥ ,
या स्वयं पद्मनाभस्य मुखपद्माद्विनिःसृता ॥
yā svayaṁ padmanābhasya mukhapadmādviniḥsṛtā .

Why go in for other elaborate scriptures, when you can chant the Gītā—the essence of all Vedic scriptures—which issued forth from the lotus mouth of Māhā-Vishnu Himself—on whose navel is the lotus of Creation.

— ॐ —

भारतामृतसर्वस्वं विष्णोर्वक्त्राद्विनिःसृतम् ।
bhāratāmṛtasarvasvaṁ viṣṇorvaktrādviniḥsṛtam ,
गीतागङ्गोदकं पीत्वा पुनर्जन्म न विद्यते ॥
gītāgaṅgodakaṁ pītvā punarjanma na vidyate .

There is no more rebirth for one who partakes of the sacred waters of the Gītā-Gangā—the holy stream which flowed out from the lotus lips of Shri Māhā-Vishnu—the nectar which is the quintessence of Māhā-Bhārata.

— ॐ —

एकं शास्त्रं देवकीपुत्रगीतमेको देवो देवकीपुत्र एव ।
ekaṁ śāstraṁ devakīputragītameko devo devakīputra eva ,
एको मन्त्रस्तस्य नामानि यानि कर्माप्येकं तस्य देवस्य सेवा ॥
eko mantrastasya nāmāni yāni karmāpyekaṁ tasya devasya sevā .

The holy Gītā of Krishna—son of Devakī—is the One Scripture; Krishna—son of Devakī—is the One God; the name Krishna—son of Devakī—is the One Mantra; service to Him—son of Devakī—is the One and only Duty.

— ॐ —

श्रीकृष्णाचरणार्पणमस्तु
śrī kṛṣṇa caraṇāarpaṇamastu
Hereby dedicated to the Lotus Feet of Bhagwāna Shri Krishna.

कायेन वाचा मनसेंद्रियैर्वा । बुद्ध्यात्मना वा प्रकृतिस्वभावात् ।
kāyena vācā manaseṁdriyairvā , buddhyātmanā vā prakritisvabhāvāt ,
करोमि यद्यत् सकलं परस्मै । नारायणायेति समर्पयामि ॥
karomi yadyat sakalaṁ parasmai , nārāyaṇāyeti samarpayāmi .

Whatever it is I do—through body, mind, speech, or sense-organs, or with my intellect and soul, or with my innate natural tendencies—whatever it be—I offer it all unto Narayana (Bhagwāna Shri Krishna / Bhagwāna Shri Rāma).

— ॐ —

या गीता सनातनस्य धर्मस्यामृतरूपिणी।
yā gītā sanātanasya dharmasyāmṛtarūpiṇī ,
लोकानां मार्गदर्शिनी तस्याः मूलं प्रयच्छामि ॥
lokānāṁ margadarśinī tasyāḥ mūlaṁ prayacchāmi .

That Gītā, which's the nectar-form of Sanātana Dharma—the guide of the worlds upon The-Path—towards Her sacred roots I now proceed to take refuge.

Be Inspired and Inspire Others. Light a Lamp of Wisdom. Start your own Gitā Classes with a Friend Today.

www.ingramcontent.com/pod-product-compliance
Lightning Source LLC
Chambersburg PA
CBHW081431070526
44586CB00020B/2548

* 9 7 8 1 9 4 5 7 3 9 5 1 4 *